SOUTHERN ROOTS

SOUTHERN ROOTS

RECIPES AND STORIES FROM MAMA DIP'S DAUGHTER

SPRING COUNCIL

Countryman Press

An Imprint of W. W. Norton & Company
Independent Publishers Since 1923

Printed in Turkey
First Edition

Manufacturing by Imak Ofset
Book design by Allison Chi
Production manager: Devon Zahn

Countryman Press
www.countrymanpress.com

An imprint of W. W. Norton & Company, Inc.
500 Fifth Avenue, New York, NY 10110
www.wwnorton.com

978-1-32411-132-0

1 2 3 4 5 6 7 8 9 0

To my mother, who held me, comforted me, laughed with me, encouraged me, and shaped me. You taught me the joy of cooking and the power of sharing meals. Thank you for inviting me into your kitchens.

Cooking by feel and taste has been a heritage among black American women since slavery, and that's the way I learned to cook.

—Mildred "Mama Dip" Council

CONTENTS

Foreword 11
Introduction 13
Timeline 22

BREAKFAST AND BRUNCH 25

Pimento Cheese Biscuits 28
Grits Casserole with Shrimp Gravy 31
Cheese Grits with Corn Kernels 32
Shrimp and Salami Egg Scramble 33
Zucchini and Tomato Frittata 34
Country Ham with Milk Gravy 35
Monte Cristo Sandwich 37
Grated Sweet Potato Pancakes 38
Banana and Chocolate Coffee Cake with Rum Glaze 41
Asparagus, Bacon, and Parmesan Omelet Pie 42
Plum and Nectarine Yogurt Bowl with Wildflower Honey Granola 47

SNACKS AND STARTERS 49

Fried Chicken Lollipops with Andalouse Sauce 50
Sweet Potato Corn Bread 54
Spiced Cocktail Peanuts 57
Cheddar Cheese Relish 58
BLT Crackers 61
Ham Terrine with Ritz Crackers 62
Hot Crab Dip 63
Sardine and Cream Cheese Spread 64
Fresh Okra Fritters 67
Ham-Stuffed Eggs 68

SOUPS AND SALADS 69

Cream of Asparagus Soup with Mushroom Ragù 70
Chilled Cucumber Soup with Smoked Salmon 74
Cream of Turnip Soup with Crispy Greens 75

Beet, Apricot, and Goat Cheese Salad 77
Watermelon Salad 78
Grape and Walnut Salad 79
Iceberg Wedges with Cucumbers and Black Forest Ham 80
Caesar Salad with Arugula and Garlic Croutons 83
Strawberry, Romaine, and Red Onion Salad 84
Asparagus and Sweet Pepper Salad 86

VEGETABLE SIDES 87

Braised Collard Greens 90
Stewed Corn 93
Tangy Potato Salad 94
Country-Fried Cabbage 95
Macaroni and Cheese 96
Apple Coleslaw 99
Purple Hull Peas and Corn 101
String Beans with Fresh Herbs 102
Spinach, Parmesan, and Artichoke Gratin 105
Onion Potatoes 106
Sweet Potato and Apple Bake 107
Brûléed Corn Pudding 108

MAINS 109

Chicken and Drop Dumplings 114
Smothered Fried Chicken with Andouille Sausage 116
Chicken Croquettes with Butter and Herb Cream Sauce 118
Fried Green Tomato Parmesan 121
Carolina Burger 122
Pinto Bean Bowl with Fatback Corn Bread Crumble and Onion Jam 124
Eggplant and Tomato Casserole 126
Braised Beef Short Ribs 129
Collards and Italian Sausage Lasagna 130
Country-Style Pork Spare Ribs 133
Pan-Fried Lamb Chops 134
Pecan and Herb-Crusted Salmon 135
Shrimp Potato Salad 136
Shrimp Croquettes with Remoulade Coleslaw on a Bun 137

HOLIDAYS AT HOME 141

Fried Walnuts 144
Mama's Grilled Corn on the Cob 146
Sweet Potato Hot Cross Buns 147
Mashed Potatoes and Turnips with Thyme Butter 149
Okra and Black-Eyed Peas Pilaf 150

Swiss Chard and Chickpea Bread and Butter Pudding 153
Corn Bread and Pickle-Crusted Bone-In Spiral Cut Ham 154
Prime Rib Roast with Yorkshire Pudding 156
Buttermilk Yeast Rolls 157
Fried Turkey with Giblet Gravy, Mortadella Corn Bread Dressing, and Cranberry Compote 161
Cucumber and Jalapeño Tea Sandwiches 168
Arugula and Egg Salad Tea Sandwiches 169
Tomato and Shrimp Butter Tea Sandwiches 170
Gorgonzola and Walnut Scones 173
Lemon Curd 174

DESSERTS 175

Coconut Cake with Coconut Sour Cream Frosting 177
Yellow Layer Cake with Pumpkin Frosting 178
Banana Pudding with Chocolate Meringue 180
Apple Crisp with Cinnamon Whipped Cream 181
Strawberry Biscuit Cake 183
Goat Cheese Pound Cake 184
Sweet Bread with Raspberries 189
Sweet Potato and Pecan Pie 191
Fresh Fruit Pineapple Upside-Down Cake 192
Oatmeal Peanut Butter Bars 193
Chocolate Cake with Caramel Pecan Fudge Frosting 196
Chocolate Bread Pudding with Candied Bacon 198
Lemon Chess Pie with Cardamom 200
Sweet Potato Custard Ice Cream 204
Ginger Snap Ice Cream 207
Cantaloupe and Raspberry Milkshake 208
Peach and Citrus Ice Cream 209
Orange Cream Punch 211

DRINKS 213

Old-Fashioned Lemonade 214
Cardamom Iced Tea 215
Peach Lemonade 216
The Big O 223
Peanut Rum and Coke 224
Big Dipper Cocktail 227
Chapel Hill Cocktail 229

Menus 231
Afterword 235
Acknowledgments 239
Index 241

FOREWORD

ANITA SPRING COUNCIL is my beloved friend and colleague. I am so moved by this poignant and joy-filled book. It is a masterpiece, strongly deserving of a place of honor among the canon of the region's best food books. Spring shares a beautifully curated collection of Council family favorite recipes side by side with her own exciting dishes, as well as sage kitchen and entertaining wisdom. Those who have been lucky guests at Spring's table know her fabulous style, a wonderful mix of elegant Southern ease enlivened by her trained eye, which recognizes one-of-a-kind artifacts at local thrift markets and vintage shops.

With Spring's voice at the fore, *Southern Roots* brings the multigenerational legacy of North Carolina's Council family into home kitchens, a rare gift from a fabled cooking heritage and its deep connection to season, place, local farming, foraging, food preservation, and story. Spring notes how recipes and cooking methods were shared orally between women in her family, creating a "common food terroir." I love Spring's childhood memory of "flavor clouds" wafting through Chapel Hill's historic African American Northside neighborhood as women prepared supper for their families. She writes, "Although Southern country cooking is a family tradition, curiosity has allowed me to preserve and evolve within my culinary heritage. At the heart of these recipes is the history of my ancestors, culminating in a diversity of flavors planted here in the South."

Integral to *Southern Roots* is the powerful impact of Black chefs, farmers, and entrepreneurs on the rise of New Southern Cuisine in Chapel Hill and Durham in the 1980s. In 1985, journalist Craig Claiborne, the former *New York Times* food editor and restaurant critic, visited the North Carolina Piedmont region where he wrote an important review of its dining scene, "Sophistication Spices Southern Food." (That phrase could serve as a subtitle for *Southern Roots*.) Claiborne ate a memorable lunch at Dip's Country Kitchen that included fried chicken, deep-fried chicken livers, pork chitlins, black-eyed peas, coleslaw, okra and tomato stew served with corn bread, and peach cobbler for dessert. Claiborne wrote, "At the places I visited, in the Winston-Salem and Chapel Hill regions, food is expertly prepared, menus are alive with imagination and there is artistry in the presentation. North Carolina still boasts some of the finest barbecue and down-home cooking to be found anywhere, but the newest establishments are marvels of sophistication."[1] Several of the dishes that Claiborne enjoyed that day are reimagined in *Southern Roots* and evoke the evolution of cooking styles, flavors, and ingredients through Spring's culinary signature.

Southern Roots is a love letter from Spring to her mother, restaurateur and cook, Mildred Edna Cotton "Mama Dip" Council, who died in 2018. Beyond her role as mother, Mama Dip was her daughter's "teacher, motivator, and mentor." Throughout the book, Spring weaves in the love given and received by Mildred Council, who fiercely protected her children from racism and poverty while teaching them to cherish their Black heritage and history.

The Council women are royalty in Chapel Hill, admired for their Southern culinary genius and their deep commitment to community service, education, and social justice. I have known three generations—Spring; her "Mama;" and Spring's accomplished daughter, baker, chef, and entrepreneur, Tonya Council. Their friendship is treasured by our family. We cannot begin to count the delicious Mama Dip's meals, porch parties at UNC's Center for the Study of the American South, student end-of-semester gatherings, birthday caramel cakes, and Tonya's cookies we have enjoyed together.

Southern Roots joins an exciting contemporary space of Black-authored cookbooks that bring Black agency and voice to Southern foodways. African and African American food traditions are the heart of the region's evolving food history, yet for centuries racist power structures marginalized Black writers, cooks, and food entrepreneurs whose labor and intellect were integral to Southern cuisine. Award-winning authors Jessica B. Harris, Vertamae Smart-Grosvenor, Edna Lewis, Toni Tipton-Martin, Leni Sorensen, Michael Twitty, and Psyche Williams-Forson led a racial reckoning within Southern foodways. This movement has grown exponentially, enriched by the work of Black writers like Mashama Bailey, Matthew Raiford, Nicole Taylor, Bryant Terry, and the recent partnership of journalist Kayla Stewart and the late Emily Meggett, a native of Edisto Island, South Carolina, and Gullah Geechee home-cooking authority.

Spring's voice heals us in these divisive times. Her reflection on the massive changes she witnessed as a young Black woman coming of age in a desegregating South reinforces my faith that the American experiment in democracy will prevail, because of families like the Councils and their beloved community who rejoiced at the welcome table they set in Chapel Hill for over fifty years. That legacy continues in the spirit-filled, joyful pages of *Southern Roots* and in the next generation of talented women entrepreneurs in the Council family.

Marcie Cohen Ferris
Professor Emeritus, American Studies
University of North Carolina at Chapel Hill

---

1 Craig Claiborne, "Sophistication Spices Southern Food," *New York Times*, June 26, 1985. https://www.nytimes.com/1985/06/26/garden/sophistication-spices-southern-food.html.

INTRODUCTION

LIKE A DISH THAT brings together different ingredients, this cookbook is a collection of stories about people and places—particularly lessons from my mother, Mildred Edna Cotton Council, affectionately known as Mama Dip. It also offers glimpses into my neighbors' kitchens and explores the influence of business owners I encountered. These food stories include a visit to a country garden, my first grown-up tea party, the cooking aromas of my neighborhood, kids foraging for summer fruit, and my mother's timeless cooking advice. The mentors who preserved their family traditions and shared them with me helped shape my path. The 100 recipes in this collection reflect both the food and cooking traditions that I grew up with, as well as my explorations into new culinary experiences.

Through the beautiful tradition of oral food sharing, delicious recipes are passed down from generation to generation, preserving family legacies along the way. This tradition extended beyond my immediate family, forging connections within the community and establishing what I like to think of as a common food terroir.

Mama was born in 1929 to Ed and Effie Cotton and, like me, was the youngest in her family. She grew up on a tenant farm in Baldwin Township, Chatham County, North Carolina, where she learned to cook. She moved to Chapel Hill, married my father, Joe Council, and helped raise a community of children (in addition to her own). She opened a successful traditional Southern cooking restaurant, Mama Dip's Kitchen—first in a rented space and then in her own building, which she also designed herself. She wrote two best-selling cookbooks, *Mama Dip's Kitchen* and *Mama Dip's Family Cookbook,* and became nationally known through her many television appearances, including *Good Morning America* and QVC. She was honored as "A Pillar of Southern Cooking" in the headline of the *New York Times* obituary that ran upon her death in 2018.

My mother had her first child at 19, and had eight children—including me, the youngest—by the time she was 27. Can you imagine having eight children born one year apart at *27 years old*? Norma, Geary, Joe Jr., William and Julia (the twins), Sandra, Annette, and me, Anita Spring Council.

My family always called me by my middle name, Spring. Aunt Marie once joked that Mama had so many children, she started naming them by the seasons.

MAMA
DIP'S
KITCHEN

Folks often ask me how I got my name. They usually think I was born in the spring, but I actually arrived eight days before the season began—on March 12, 1957. Mama liked the name of the American actress Spring Byington. In school, I went by Anita until we were given the option to choose what we wanted to be called. To end the confusion between my home name and my school name, I chose Spring.

BILL'S BAR-B-Q, ESTABLISHED 1957

That same year, my family's restaurant journey began—rooted in Northside, historically the largest African American community in Chapel Hill, where some families have lived for eight generations. Northside is my nucleus—where my mental, physical, and culinary growth began. It's where I discovered my connection with nature, where I put down the kickball to pick up a book and read on our porch. It's where my palate developed, where my love for cooking emerged, and where I first beheld the beauty of a well-set table.

Northside also holds my mother's dream of owning her own restaurant and is where my career began.

North Graham Street, off the west end of Franklin Street, was the heart of Chapel Hill's Black community, with a laundromat, funeral home, barber shop, beauty salons, corner store, billiard room, fine dining nightclub, and motel. My paternal grandfather, Bill Minor, worked in a lumberyard for many years and saved enough money to build his small, fast-casual restaurant in this Northside neighborhood. In 1957, the year I was born, Grandpa Bill opened Bill's Bar-B-Q.

It was primarily a take-out operation, but there was a small counter with four round stools where freshly prepared food was served using quality ingredients. My grandfather hired a menu developer (my mother), short-order cooks, a pitmaster, and delivery drivers. He sourced ingredients from local Black farmers and fishermen from the North Carolina coast.

Fish Friday was a highlight—pogies, black bass, and spots were butterflied, coated in cornmeal, deep-fried until golden brown, and served between two slices of white bread. Flounder, with three scored lines on the skin-side, was fried and served in a box with french fries, coleslaw, and hush puppies.

Bill's Bar-B-Q's real chicken sandwiches were simple but special: two bone-in pieces of chicken (white or dark meat) sandwiched between two slices of white bread. What made it stand out was the way you ate it. Tear off a piece of bread the size of a cracker to use as an eating utensil, break off a piece of chicken, and you have a piping hot piece of deliciousness, a moist and crispy mouthful. The white bread soaked up a little oil from the fried chicken, and bits of the crispy crumbs would attach to it, too. No fork, no knife—just fingers and a napkin and a piece of bread made it happen.

Bill's Bar-B-Q was known for many dishes, including barbecue sandwiches, hot dogs, chuckwagons—chicken-fried steak seasoned with a spicy batter, served on an oversized hamburger bun with mayonnaise, lettuce, and tomato—Carolina burgers, bowls of pinto beans topped with chopped onions and hush puppies, grilled honey buns with a scoop of vanilla ice cream, and homemade pies.

There were non-carbonated orange and grape drinks in waxed cartons, and customers loved drinking chocolate milk with their meal as much as they enjoyed soft drinks. Bill's had its own language. If a customer requested a hot dog "all the way," that meant mustard, onions, slaw, and homemade chili.

Last but not least, there were the box assemblers: my sisters and me. My first unofficial job was making hundreds of "chicken boxes." My grandfather had a large storage room dedicated to take-out box assembly. He never needed to ask us to make the boxes. We'd go to the room, pull the long string hanging from the light fixture to illuminate it, and count the inventory of boxes stacked high on the long table, restocking as needed. We did not waste time, motivated by the cash we earned and the fried chicken sandwich that was part of our pay—a delicious lunch.

Growing up around Grandpa Bill's restaurant taught me that food is more than just nourishment and flavor; it could also bring in coins. Food meant money for swimming, cash for snacks, change for comic books, coins for the gumball machine with the plastic containers filled with a toy (that took a miracle for one to be released into your hand), and coins for the jukebox.

The jukebox played an essential role in the restaurant, enlivening the atmosphere with its songs. Customers would snap their fingers, sing, and sway to the music while waiting for their orders. The clinking sound as the dime rolled down into the selection mechanism, the movement of the exchange of the 45 rpm record from its slot onto the spinning disk, and the slight scratching sound of the needle on the edge of the vinyl before making its way onto the record grooves all signaled that a song—usually about love—was about to play. In 1964, James Brown's "I Got You (I Feel Good)" and The Drifters' "Up on the Roof" filled the air, and 1965 brought the Four Tops' "I Can't Help Myself" and The Temptations' "My Girl."

My grandfather was a hardworking community leader. He provided meals for the protesters when Martin Luther King Jr. visited Chapel Hill for a meeting at the Robeson Street Center on North Robeson Street, now known as Hargraves Community Center, just north of Mama Dip's Kitchen. Grandpa Bill did not drive fancy cars or dress to the nines. His focus was always on taking care of his family and providing jobs for the community. He ran the business for 11 years before retiring in 1968.

BILL'S BAR-B-Q, ESTABLISHED 1969

When Grandpa Bill stepped away from the restaurant, my family's spirit of entrepreneurship continued and evolved. In 1968, my father purchased a white Chevrolet

Step-Van and started a home-based food truck business, primarily serving construction sites around the UNC campus. Every morning, before heading to her job at UNC Hospital, Mama would prepare the food: breakfast biscuits, barbecue sandwiches, pies, and cakes. I was part of the kitchen cleanup team, responsible for washing dishes and helping wherever I was needed.

Our neighbor, Mrs. Charlie Mae, was hired to help as the business grew. Mama would fuss about how we did our job poorly, and Mrs. Charlie Mae, standing at the sink, would back her up like an amen corner in church: *Yes Dip, you are right, Dip.* One morning, I'd had enough. I told Mama I was tired of hearing it. As soon as the last word left my mouth, I ran out the back door like an Olympic sprinter hearing the starter's pistol. Once I got to the street, I looked around and saw her chasing after me and heard her shouting for me to come back. I kept running!

Then, salvation! My sister called out that Mama's taxi had arrived to take her to work. I got on the school bus. In each of my seven classes at school, I thought about going home and facing the consequences. Was I going to be told that I could not go to the school dance and/or was it going to be a long, long lecture on respect? When I got home, I made myself invisible. But to my surprise, Mama had prepared one of my favorite meals: lasagna, tossed salad, and garlic bread. She never mentioned my wrongdoing. Knowing my mother, she probably thought about it at work, told the story to her coworkers, and laughed about it.

The next day, I went to visit my friends two houses down, and their mother said, "I was on the porch and saw Spring running, and then I saw Dip running behind her in her slip." That is all I heard about it. I learned a valuable lesson that day: consider your words.

By 1969, my parents had saved enough money to reopen Bill's-Bar-B-Q in Grandpa's original location, using the restaurant as a base for the food truck and offering a delivery service to UNC students. The menu expanded. Mama added breakfast—country ham, bacon, or sausage, with eggs cooked to order, grits, biscuits, or toast—along with lunch and dinner plates of meat or fish with two sides.

Our food truck business thrived, expanding to more job sites, including Triem, an assembly-line operation in Carrboro where my father made morning, lunch, and afternoon break stops. In the summer of 1971, my sister Lane (16) and I (14) took over running the truck. Lane drove, and I assisted her with serving the customers. Our biggest stop was the OWASA water tank construction project on Nunn Mountain off Piney Mountain Road. The workers, many from different states, always had requests—anything from chewing tobacco, a particular brand of cigarettes, a favorite type of gum. We would tell our dad, and by the next workday, he would have it stocked.

During those years, I missed out on hanging out with friends, ball games, and school dances. But what I did achieve from working was my own weekly paycheck. I learned early that having a job and showing up every day builds character, self-reliance, endurance, courage, and confidence. And when life threw its hardest challenges my way, I drew strength from those lessons, the same way I drew strength from the meals we served—hot, homemade, and made with care.

DIP'S COUNTRY KITCHEN, ESTABLISHED 1976

During a 1994 oral history interview with the journal *Southern Cultures,* Mama said, "I think the biggest turning point in my life was when I left my husband." True to her word, she left a year after I graduated—just as she always said she would once her youngest finished high school. That moment marked a new beginning, not just for Mama, but for me, as well.

She left our family business and, on November 15, 1976, started one of her own, naming it Dip's Country Kitchen. Each morning, she dropped me off at Bill's Bar-B-Q, where I continued to work, before driving two blocks to her new place on Rosemary Street in downtown Chapel Hill. One day, while working, I daydreamed about my mother being alone at her new restaurant. The next day, within minutes of her dropping me off, instead of going into the building, I walked to Dip's Country Kitchen and joined her at her new business.

It was a change for me and a new learning experience. At Bill's, I had been a short-order cook and cashier, but at her new restaurant, I became a waitress. It did not take long for me to adjust to waiting on tables thanks to my experience at Bill's, and because I had also spent time with Mama in my youth when she worked as a waitress and cook at Thurman Atkins' Hollywood Grill. We did not speak much about my leaving Bill's Bar-B-Q. She only asked me if I was going back there, and my answer was no.

And so, the two of us started out on our new journey. Mama would send me to our local grocer, Fowler's Food Store, to replenish ingredients and supplies, and I was responsible for taking care of the dining room. Local farmers heard about Mama's cooking, and they would drive up and park at the restaurant's front door. She would go out to greet them, taste and sniff their fruits and vegetables, and then make a purchase. The farmers brought watermelons, corn, string beans, collard greens, field peas, squash, turnip greens, peaches, apples, pears, blueberries, sweet potatoes, and scuppernong grapes—which we ate as a snack.

The business started off with just a few customers trickling in. Many days, we sat in silence at a booth by the window—watching the 5 PM traffic pass by. As we sat in our usual spot, I recall saying to myself, *Folks do not know what is in this building—they do not know the delicious food Mama is cooking.*

Later, employees from a local newspaper started frequenting our restaurant. One writer said she wanted to write an article about Dip's Country Kitchen. It took almost a year before it happened, but to our surprise, when the article finally ran, it was on the front page. That was the turning

point. Then, the Chapel Hill community came to eat and discovered for themselves what was inside—getting a taste of the food Mama learned to cook on her family farm.

On June 26, 1985, we got another surprise: the *New York Times* food critic Craig Claiborne included Dip's Country Kitchen in a roundup review of North Carolina dining establishments, calling it "a genuine, no-frills restaurant." We did not know much about food critics at the time and how much impact his words would have on expanding our clientele. I didn't quite understand what all the hype was about. To me, Mama was cooking the delicious food we grew up eating.

But one day, while serving a family of six, the mother thanked me for being nice. She explained that her mother had recently passed away, and they came to Mama Dip's Kitchen because we served the same food her mother used to cook. That's when it hit me—why the media was so interested in Mama's cooking.

Mama always added dishes to her menu based on what customers requested. At first, we served bowls of Brunswick stew along with barbecue and rib dinners, but when customers wanted a combination of the two, she satisfied their request and added a Brunswick stew with barbecue and a chicken and rib dinner. There were times when cakes were still warm from just being frosted, and pies were too hot to cut, but the customer wanted a slice, so they would wait a bit for the desserts to cool down enough to be sliced. Mama was happy doing what she loved—cooking traditional country fare, greeting her customers, and visiting with the farmers. Her goal was to please her customers, and she did an excellent job.

Mama's impact went far beyond just satisfying her diners. She invited entire elementary school classes, creating a special place for them to dine and ensuring that kids who may not have had the opportunity to eat at a full-service restaurant were able to do so. She also created a space for adults struggling with drug addiction, offering them both jobs and encouragement. She received many letters from male inmates in the local prison who wanted the opportunity to join other inmates working at her restaurant in the work release program. She did not hesitate to take action when important community issues arose. For example, she went before the Chapel Hill Town Council and successfully argued that the speed limit on the west end of Rosemary Street should be reduced from 35 to 25 miles per hour.

Both the Mildred Council Annual Community Dinner and a charitable foundation bear her name.

Mama also foresaw the threats to Northside, even before they began to take shape. She recognized that the centrally located land, rich with history and community, was becoming an attractive property for investors and developers. Plans for mixed-use, multistory developments aimed for UNC students, along with luxury apartments and condominiums for those who like the leisurely lifestyle and convenience of living downtown, were on the horizon. She understood that these plans threatened to alter the fabric of our fragile neighborhood.

As my siblings and I grew into adulthood, Mama touched many folks' lives in her Black community and brought that same love to her employees and customers at Mama Dip's Kitchen. I know this because of the outpouring of love and support we received from customers near and far after her passing. When Mama could no longer drive her red Toyota pickup truck to the farmers' market or go to her restaurant to do what she loved most, cook for and greet her customers, I started going to the Carrboro Farmers' Market each week, bringing Mama a bouquet to remind her of the connections she had created there. She appreciated my getting her flowers, which I'd buy whenever they were in season at the market, and she would ask me to place them in one of her antique vases and place the bouquet in the center of her dresser near the family photos and greeting cards she received from family and friends.

Returning to the market after my mother's death in May 2018 was a bit difficult because I did not want to reveal my sad emotions, which were between me and God, who was keeping me strong through His words and prayer. But I knew I had to go back. On a sunny spring day with a gentle breeze, I took my first step into the market. I held back my tears and braced for the greetings and condolences I would receive from the farmers and shoppers. I left the market with a "boatload" of fixings, including asparagus, turnips, strawberries, carrots, arugula, lettuce, onions, cabbage, garlic, spinach, and, of course, flowers.

Most importantly, I left there feeling much better, *I had found closure,* a sense of peace, a sense of place, and a desire to return weekly, letting the ingredients from the soil from local farmers be stirred in my pots and pans, baked in my oven, and tossed in my salad recipes, giving me a sense of Mama's presence in my kitchen and bringing back memories of the times the two of us spent together in her red pickup truck, enjoying visits to farmers' markets, gardening shops, and pick-your-own blueberry and strawberry farms and, of course, in Dip's Country Kitchen.

While developing the recipes in this book, I embraced traditional Southern cooking and created dishes that emerged from my expanded food terroir, and I held my childhood food memories near as I seasoned, tasted, and added more seasoning until I obtained the tasty flavors that pleased my palate. The recipes included in *Southern Roots* reach beyond my home, neighborhood, county, and state into other regions of the South with influences from the traditional foods brought here by immigrant families from varied countries and cultures. Although Southern country cooking is a family tradition, curiosity has allowed me to preserve and evolve within my culinary heritage. At the heart of these recipes is the history of my ancestors, culminating in a diversity of flavors planted here in the South.

TIMELINE

1929
My mother, Mildred Edna Cotton, later known as Mildred "Mama Dip" Council, was born in Chatham County, North Carolina. Her early years in the rural South laid the foundation for her deep connection to food, family, and community.

1945
Hargraves Community Center, originally known as the Negro Community Center, opened in Chapel Hill's historically African American neighborhood, Northside. This center would become a cornerstone of the community, fostering opportunities for social gatherings, education, and cultural pride.

1957–1968
My paternal grandparents, Bill and Mary Minor, owned and operated Bill's Bar-B-Q, a small, fast-casual eatery on North Graham Street in Chapel Hill's Northside African American business district. This restaurant was more than a place to eat—it was a hub for fellowship and a symbol of resilience in a segregated society.

1957
I was born in Chapel Hill, North Carolina, and named Anita Spring Council. As the youngest of eight children of Mildred "Mama Dip" and Joe Council, I grew up surrounded by family, food, and stories that shaped my identity.

1960
Inspired by the Greensboro lunch counter sit-ins, the Chapel Hill Nine, including my cousin Albert Williams, organized sit-ins at Chapel Hill's Colonial Drug Store. Their courage in the fight for civil rights became a source of pride and inspiration for our family.

That same year, Martin Luther King Jr. visited Chapel Hill, further galvanizing the community's commitment to justice and equality.

1966
Chapel Hill public schools were desegregated, marking a new chapter for the town's African American youth. As a child witnessing this transition, I saw both the struggles and the opportunities it brought.

1968
I worked at Chapel Hill Public Library, where I discovered the transformative power of literature. Works by Langston Hughes, Gwendolyn Brooks, and Richard Wright opened my eyes to the richness of African American culture and storytelling.

1969
My parents reopened Bill's Bar-B-Q with an expanded menu, blending traditional family recipes with new creations that resonated with the community. My sister Lane (16) and I (14) managed the food truck operation—a challenging yet rewarding experience that taught us responsibility and the art of customer service.

1976
My mother left Bill's Bar-B-Q to pursue her dream of opening her own restaurant. In a rented space on Rosemary Street, she launched Dip's Country Kitchen, where her warmth and culinary talent drew customers from all walks of life. I joined her in this new venture, eager to help her bring her vision to life.

1985
Craig Claiborne, the renowned food critic for the *New York Times*, discovered Dip's Country Kitchen and featured it in a roundup review of Chapel Hill restaurants. This recognition brought national attention to my mother's cooking and elevated our small restaurant to a new level of success.

1996
Customers referred to her as Mama Dip, so she decided to change the name of the restaurant from Dip's Country Kitchen to Mama Dip's Kitchen.

My mother established the first Annual Community Dinner, a gathering that celebrated togetherness and shared purpose. After her passing, it was renamed the Mildred Council Annual Community Dinner in her honor.

1998
Mama Dip's product line was developed, bringing her signature flavors into homes across the country. From sauces to baked goods, these products allowed more people to experience her cooking.

1999
Mama Dip's Kitchen moved into its own freestanding building, designed and owned by my mother. This milestone marked her triumph as a Black entrepreneur and a beacon of perseverance and vision.

Mama Dip's Kitchen Cookbook was published by University of North Carolina Press, sharing her recipes and stories with a wider audience. It became a bestseller, selling over 246,000 copies and cementing her legacy in the culinary world.

2001
My mother made her first appearance on the QVC home shopping channel, where her charm and authenticity won over viewers and further expanded her brand.

2005
Mama Dip's Family Cookbook was published, featuring even more recipes and family stories that celebrated our traditions.

2007
The Marian Cheek Jackson Center for Saving and Making History was founded in Chapel Hill's Northside community, preserving the history and culture of the area that had shaped so much of our family's story.

2009
My sister, Annette "Neecy" Council, founded Sweet Neecy Cake Mix Company.

2012
My daughter, Tonya Council, founded Tonya's Cookies.

2017
Tonya opened Sweet Tea & Cornbread, a retail store offering gourmet southern foods and products originating in North Carolina in Raleigh's Crabtree Valley Mall.

2018
My mother passed away, leaving behind an extraordinary legacy. In her *New York Times* obituary, she was remembered as "A Pillar of Southern Cooking," a testament to her enduring impact on food and community.

2019
Tonya acquired NC Made, an online destination for artisanal food and gifts.

2021
Tonya's Pecan Crisp Cookies were named on Oprah Winfrey's "Favorite Things" holiday list.

2022
My niece, Erika Council, opened Bomb Biscuit Company in Atlanta, carrying on the family tradition of culinary excellence. Her cookbook, *Still We Rise*, was published in 2023.

2023
Tonya opened Tonya's Cookies, a bakery in Chapel Hill, North Carolina.

2024
Mama Dip's Kitchen closed for dine-in service but continues as a brand, ensuring that my mother's legacy lives on through products and stories.

Tonya opened Tonya's Café next to her bakery, focusing on her sense of tradition with a modern edge.

My sisters and I received Lifetime Achievement Awards from Southern Foodways Alliance, a recognition of our family's contributions to Southern food and culture.

BREAKFAST AND BRUNCH

Mama's Cooking Lessons

MAMA WAS A SUPERHERO, but delicate in her approach to the job. Taste was her true superpower. I watched her sample tastes throughout the cooking process, and saw how her nose assisted in capturing the deliciousness of her dishes. How else could she put out such tasty dishes, so gratifying that they were memorable? Away from her table, my mind conjured images of her rich gravies, the crispiness of her fry, and the aroma of her kitchen. I never once heard her say she was tired of cooking, even after a full day on the job. She displayed a childlike manner while cooking, just like her nine-year-old self when her papa—for the first time—told her that it was her turn to prepare the meal, giving her the chance to create and share all she had learned.

She reminisced about her older sister Bernice and family friend Roland Norwood—how they fried, baked, stewed, braised, and boiled the fruits and vegetables they grew and the animals they raised on their Southern farm. Mama was responsible for bringing in the wood for the stove and watching the steam rise from a pot of boiling water—an indicator of how the fire was burning—so she could add more wood as needed. Alongside Bernice and Roland, she learned to cook with all her senses—smelling, watching, listening, touching, and tasting throughout the process.

Looking back on the way Mama welcomed me and my siblings into her kitchen, I now realize that, as a curious child, I didn't grasp that she was preserving her heritage by teaching us to cook through oral tradition. Her repertoire of recipes and flavors was not written on note cards or kept in a recipe box—it lived in her mind, taste buds, and heart, and was conveyed to us directly. It wasn't until later that she committed the recipes to cookbooks.

Mama's kitchen was where I felt loved, where I was happy to sit at the table, to listen and learn through leisure and curiosity. I relished being there, and my fondest memories reside in those moments. Because of this, I feel a deep desire to re-create the warm, gratifying atmosphere she cultivated and to share the talents she passed on to me.

Mama taught us to create recipes using sight, taste, touch, and aroma, working at the central table where we prepared meals and ate together. The table was where she unloaded groceries, made cakes and frostings, canned fruits and vegetables, and served our plated meals—always a protein, a vegetable, and a starch—to nourish us. She told stories, shared ingredient knowledge, hummed songs, and drew us into her kitchen to watch as she prepared our family meals.

This is the house where my mother learned to cook.

Mama "dump cooked" (cooking without measuring utensils) and offered tastings as she added ingredients and seasonings. I learned that being in the kitchen with my mother was a time of connection when we had her undivided attention. Mama found satisfaction in teaching us, and during those daily meals and holiday feasts, I would float around her kitchen attached to her apron strings.

Dump cooking, tasting, smelling, and touching—watching raw ingredients transform into a finished dish—bonded us during those times in her kitchen.

Mama often spoke about leaving a legacy for her children and grandchildren. As part of that legacy, I'm on a mission to share the story of my time in Mama's kitchens and within our community—particularly, but not only, Chapel Hill's African American food scene.

PIMENTO CHEESE BISCUITS

Stuff these moist and flaky biscuits with egg salad, ham, or sliced tomato, or eat them plain.

MAKES 12 BISCUITS

2 cups self-rising flour
1 teaspoon baking powder
½ teaspoon salt
1 (3-ounce) package cream cheese, cold and cut into cubes
2 tablespoons unsalted butter, cold and cut into cubes
½ cup grated cheddar cheese
2 tablespoons diced pimentos, well drained
½ cup milk

Preheat the oven to 425°F.

Whisk together the flour, baking powder, and salt in a large bowl. Using a pastry cutter or your fingertips, cut in the cream cheese, butter, and cheddar cheese until pea-sized lumps form. Add the pimentos and milk to the flour mixture. Work everything together until a soft dough forms.

Turn the dough out onto a lightly floured surface. Roll out the dough until it is ½ inch thick. With a floured 2-inch cookie cutter, cut the dough into rounds. Place the rounds on a lightly greased baking sheet. Bake for 15 to 20 minutes, or until golden brown.

GRITS CASSEROLE

WITH SHRIMP GRAVY

This version of shrimp and grits keeps well on a buffet. The flavors are simply mouthwatering.

SERVES 6

FOR THE CASSEROLE

3 cups water

1 cup stone-ground grits, uncooked

3 tablespoons butter

1 cup grated white cheddar cheese

1 cup milk

3 eggs, beaten

FOR THE SHRIMP GRAVY

4 slices bacon

1 cup diced onion

2 garlic cloves, finely minced

¼ cup all-purpose flour

2 cups hot water

1½ pounds shrimp, peeled and deveined

2 tablespoons chopped Italian parsley

TO MAKE THE CASSEROLE

Preheat the oven to 350°F.

Lightly butter a medium baking dish. Bring the water to a boil in a large saucepan. Stir in the grits. Reduce the heat and simmer, stirring frequently for 5 to 6 minutes, or until the liquid has been absorbed.

Remove from the heat. Add the butter and cheese, and stir until the cheese and butter melt. Let the grits cool completely. Stir the milk and eggs into the cooled grits. Pour the grits mixture into a baking dish. Bake for 25 to 30 minutes, or until the center is set.

TO MAKE THE SHRIMP GRAVY

Cook the bacon in a large skillet until it is crispy. Remove the bacon and pour off all the fat except 1 tablespoon. Crumble the bacon and set it aside.

Add the onion and garlic to the skillet and sauté until the onion is soft. Stir the flour into the skillet until the flour absorbs the fat. Gradually whisk the water into the flour mixture and continue whisking until the mixture is smooth, 3 to 5 minutes.

Add the shrimp. Continue cooking until the shrimp turns pink and the gravy is thickened and bubbly. Pour the shrimp gravy over the grits casserole and garnish with the crumbled bacon and parsley.

CHEESE GRITS
WITH CORN KERNELS

Grits are a staple breakfast in the South. The corn gives the grits a hint of sweetness as well as a slight crunch.

SERVES 8

- 4 cups water
- ½ teaspoon salt
- 1 cup grits
- 1 cup corn kernels
- 2 tablespoons unsalted butter
- ½ cup grated Parmesan cheese

In a medium saucepan, bring the water and salt to a boil. Gradually stir in the grits. Reduce the heat to low. Cook the grits uncovered for 10 minutes, stirring occasionally. Stir in the corn kernels and cook for an additional 5 minutes, or until the grits are done and the water is absorbed. Add the butter and Parmesan. Stir until the butter and cheese are melted.

SHRIMP AND SALAMI EGG SCRAMBLE

I discovered the tasty combination of shrimp and salami when I was in need of breakfast and had leftover salami from a party. Adding cream cheese brings a creamy texture and flavor to this dish. The best recipes can be created from clearing out the refrigerator.

SERVES 6

- 2 tablespoons unsalted butter
- ¼ pound shrimp, shelled and deveined, cut into bite-size pieces
- 8 slices salami, diced
- 8 eggs, well beaten
- 2 ounces cream cheese, cut into cubes

Melt the butter in a medium skillet over medium-low heat. Add the shrimp and salami, and sauté until the shrimp turns pink.

Reduce the heat to low. Pour the eggs into the skillet and let them sit until they begin to set on the bottom, about 30 seconds. Scramble the eggs until they look creamy. Sprinkle the cream cheese over the eggs and stir until melted, making sure that the eggs do not become dry. Serve immediately.

ZUCCHINI AND TOMATO FRITTATA

The combination of zucchini, tomato, and feta cheese gives this moist and delicious frittata a wonderful flavor.

SERVES 6

- 8 eggs, well beaten
- ¼ cup milk
- 2 tablespoons chopped fresh basil
- ¼ teaspoon salt
- ½ teaspoon freshly ground black pepper
- ½ cup olive oil
- 1 cup feta cheese
- ½ pound zucchini, sliced into ½-inch rounds
- 1 (10-ounce) package grape tomatoes, cut in half lengthwise

Preheat the oven to 350°F.

Whisk together the eggs, milk, basil, salt, and pepper in a large bowl.

Heat the olive oil in an oven-proof medium skillet. Pour the egg mixture into the skillet. Crumble the feta over the egg mixture and lay the zucchini and tomatoes on top. Cook until the edges begin to bubble and set, about 5 minutes. Place the skillet in the oven and cook the frittata just until the center is puffy, 20 to 25 minutes.

COUNTRY HAM
WITH MILK GRAVY

Smooth and creamy milk gravy mellows the saltiness of the country ham, and brown sugar gives this dish a caramel flavor. Serve for breakfast or have breakfast for dinner. Add baked apples, grits, and butter biscuits to complete the meal, just like my daddy served it.

SERVES 4

- 4 slices of cured country ham, cut ¼ inch thick
- 2 teaspoons vegetable oil
- ½ cup half-and-half
- 1 teaspoon light brown sugar

Soak the ham in cold water for 30 minutes to remove any excess saltiness. Pat dry with paper towels.

Coat a medium skillet with oil and place it over medium heat. Lay the ham slices in the skillet in one layer. Fry the ham 1 or 2 pieces at a time, frying each piece for 2 to 3 minutes on each side. Remove the ham pieces from the skillet and drain them on paper towels. Keep them warm.

Stir the half-and-half into the pan drippings. Add the brown sugar and stir until the sugar dissolves. Let simmer for 5 minutes. Place the ham on a platter, pour the milk gravy over it, or serve the gravy on the side.

MONTE CRISTO SANDWICH

The Monte Cristo is a delicious sandwich and fun to make. For an authentic sandwich, dust with powdered sugar as a finishing touch before serving.

SERVES 4

½ cup milk
2 eggs, well beaten
8 slices crusty bread
¼ cup mayonnaise
8 slices Swiss cheese
4 slices roasted turkey
4 slices Virginia ham
Vegetable oil for frying
Confectioners' sugar (optional)
Jam or preserves

Beat together the milk and eggs in a shallow bowl. Set aside.

Spread the slices of bread on one side with mayonnaise. Lay a slice of cheese over the mayonnaise. Top with a slice of turkey, ham, and another slice of cheese. Top each with the remaining slices of bread and press together. Set aside.

Lightly dip each sandwich into the milk mixture to coat and squeeze out any excess liquid; place on a baking sheet. Heat the oil in a large skillet over medium heat. Working two at a time, using a spatula, gently place the sandwiches in the oil. Cook 2 to 3 minutes on both sides until golden brown. Drain on paper towels. Repeat with the remaining sandwiches.

Cut each sandwich in half. Serve immediately or reheat in a 375°F oven for 10 minutes. Finish with a light sprinkle of confectioners' sugar on top and serve with your favorite jam or preserves.

GRATED SWEET POTATO PANCAKES

My inspiration for these flavorful pancakes was the grated sweet potato pudding that is served as a dessert at my family's holiday table.

SERVES 6

- 2 cups all-purpose flour
- 4 teaspoons baking powder
- ¼ teaspoon salt
- ½ teaspoon cinnamon
- 2 tablespoons sugar
- 3 eggs, well beaten
- 1 (13.5-ounce) can coconut milk
- ¼ cup milk
- 4 tablespoons unsalted butter, melted
- 2 medium sweet potatoes, peeled and grated (about 1 pound)
- ½ cup golden raisins, chopped
- 1 teaspoon vanilla extract
- Vegetable oil to coat the griddle

Preheat the griddle to medium heat.

In a medium bowl, sift together the flour, baking powder, salt, cinnamon, and sugar. Create a well in the center. Add the eggs, coconut milk, milk, and butter. Stir together until just combined. Fold in the sweet potatoes, raisins, and vanilla extract.

Coat the griddle with vegetable oil. Pour ¼ cup of batter for each pancake onto the griddle. Cook for 2 to 3 minutes on each side.

MY FATHER, THE COOK

MY FATHER'S NAME WAS Joe Council. When you have a mother like Mama Dip, people don't often ask about your dad. But in our African American Chapel Hill community, folks knew him well. He was a generous man, just like my mother—always helping others without saying a word about it. I didn't fully grasp the extent of his kindness until I was grown, when people he had quietly helped over the years told me of his good deeds.

Before I tell you about my dad's favorite weekly meal, I have to share a story about his favorite cut of steak: the ribeye.

One night, my siblings and I were in the den, enjoying our usual after-dinner TV routine. During commercial breaks, we played a game—whoever guessed the product first won a point. No prize, just bragging rights. Before sitting down, Daddy gave us a firm warning: Once he placed his steak on the coffee table, the game was over. He wanted silence!

The table was rickety and on its last leg—literally. The moment he pressed his knife into that peppery, buttery, beefy ribeye, the table collapsed like a set of pickup sticks. Without a word, he kicked the broken pieces aside, gathered them up, walked through the kitchen, and tossed them straight out the back door. Then, he left at once to find a replacement for his steak dinner. As soon as the door shut behind him, we couldn't hold it in any longer—we burst out laughing. The next week, there was a brand-new coffee table in its place.

One fall evening, Daddy came home with brown paper grocery bags filled with provisions, creating a new weekly tradition. He walked past us in the den, and soon we heard the rustling of paper bags, mixing bowls landing on the table, the cast-iron skillet clanking on the stovetop burner, and the sounds of grating, slicing, and boiling. The squeaky oven door opened and closed. The smoky, salty scent of country ham filled the house.

That's when we learned that every Thursday night, Daddy would be cooking breakfast for dinner. The menu never changed: smoky country ham, buttery cheese grits, cinnamon-baked apples, and butter biscuits. It was a meal we looked forward to all week. And it was good to see Daddy in the kitchen, showing us his culinary skills, and giving Mama a much-deserved break.

BANANA AND CHOCOLATE COFFEE CAKE WITH RUM GLAZE

This mouthwatering coffee cake is the perfect way to use up those ripe bananas. Brimming with a delightful blend of sweet fruit, rich chocolate, and a hint of rum, this cake offers an irresistible flavor combination that'll have you coming back for seconds.

SERVES 12

- 1¾ cups sugar
- 1 cup (2 sticks) unsalted butter, melted
- ¼ cup olive oil
- 3 eggs
- 3 cups all-purpose flour
- 1 teaspoon baking soda
- 1 teaspoon salt
- 1 teaspoon cinnamon
- 4 medium firm-ripe bananas (about 1 pound), sliced
- 1 cup semi-sweet chocolate chips
- ¾ cup (1½ sticks) unsalted butter
- 1 cup brown sugar
- ¼ cup heavy cream
- 2 tablespoons Myers's Rum

Preheat the oven to 350°F.

Grease and flour a 12-cup Bundt pan. In a mixing bowl, combine the sugar, melted butter, olive oil, and eggs. Beat until well blended.

In a separate medium bowl, sift together the flour, baking soda, salt, and cinnamon, and add them to the sugar mixture and mix until combined. Fold the bananas and chocolate chips into the batter, then pour the batter into the prepared Bundt pan.

Bake the cake for 60 to 65 minutes, or until a toothpick inserted into the middle of the cake comes out clean.

Prepare the glaze 5 minutes before the cake is done. In a saucepan, stir together the ¾ cup butter, brown sugar, heavy cream, and rum until the butter melts. Bring to a boil over medium heat, stirring constantly. Cook for 1 minute.

Pour the glaze over the cake while it's still in the pan. Use a small spatula or butter knife to loosen the edge of the cake so the glaze will run down the side of the cake. Let the cake cool completely. Invert the cake onto a plate so the glazed side is on top.

ASPARAGUS, BACON, AND PARMESAN OMELET PIE

Parmesan cheese and bacon pair well with the sweet flavor of asparagus in this omelet in a pie crust, imparting a delicious sweet and salty combination. This recipe is ideally served for breakfast, brunch, or lunch.

SERVES 6

FOR THE FILLING

- 1½ pounds asparagus, trimmed
- 4 thick slices of bacon, diced
- 8 eggs
- ¼ cup milk
- ¼ cup grated Parmesan cheese
- ¼ cup chopped fresh Italian parsley
- ½ cup soft bread crumbs
- 1 unbaked 9-inch pie shell (recipe follows)

FOR THE PIE CRUST

- 1 cup all-purpose flour
- ½ teaspoon salt
- 6 tablespoons unsalted butter, cold
- 3 tablespoons ice-cold water

TO MAKE THE FILLING

Preheat the oven to 375°F.

Slice the asparagus 1-inch thick on the diagonal, leaving the tips whole.

Fry the bacon in a medium skillet on medium-high heat until it is crispy, 3 to 5 minutes, stirring occasionally. Drain on paper towels and set it aside.

Beat the eggs and milk together in a large bowl. Add the Parmesan cheese, asparagus, bacon, parsley, and bread crumbs. Stir to combine.

TO MAKE THE PIE CRUST

In a medium bowl, whisk together the flour and salt. Cut in the butter with a pastry cutter until coarse crumbs form. Add the water and mix everything together to form a soft dough.

Gather the dough, press it into a ball, and then flatten it into a disk. Cover with plastic wrap and refrigerate for at least 15 minutes or up to 2 days.

Remove the dough from the refrigerator. Lightly flour a work surface and roll half of the dough out into a ⅛-inch-thick round. Press the dough into a 9-inch pie plate. Place in the refrigerator until ready to use.

TO ASSEMBLE

Pour the filling mixture into the pie shell and bake for 25 to 30 minutes, or until it is puffy in the center.

LET'S GO FORAGING

IN MY NORTHSIDE NEIGHBORHOOD, there were about 24 kids on McMasters Street at the end of Church Street, and we loved to play and have adventures outdoors. Our summer playgrounds were the wooded trail behind our homes, which led to Umstead Park to the north and Northside Elementary School just a block down the street to the south. During the "harvest season," we would split into small, mixed-aged groups and go on "hunting trips" to find fruit and nut trees in the surrounding woods and our neighbors' yards. We'd pick fruit from the trees, gather what had fallen to the ground, and leave the remaining fruit to ripen for later harvest.

The one exception was a pear tree that belonged to our neighbor, Mrs. Charlie Mae. Her tree stood there on full display, loaded with pears, and we would eat them while they were still green and hard. To stop us from eating her pears, Mrs. Charlie Mae dusted them with a white powder and sent word to every kid in the neighborhood that she had poisoned the pears, along with a more humane message that eating the pears would make us sick. When I got the message, I thought, *Surely Mrs. Charlie Mae would not poison us.* So I stepped outside to investigate—to see if it was true—and I saw what looked like flour clinging to the pears, as high as she could throw it to the top of the tree. It worked as a deterrent, for a while, until it rained. But Mrs. Charlie Mae was persistent, keeping watch from her window, and yelling, "Get away from my pear tree!" whenever she saw a small hand reaching out to grab a pear. She had reason to be so protective—she was waiting for the fruit to ripen so she could make preserves and dried pear cobblers.

Often, we would wander to our neighbors' homes, especially Ed Caldwell Jr.'s place on Church Street, which had muscadine grape arbors in the backyard and pecan trees in the front yard. Those pecans filled our bellies in the fall, and the huge tree provided cool shade in the summer. My grandparents' home on North Graham Street had apple trees; my grandmother used them to make apple pie for their restaurant, Bill's Bar-B-Q. Miss Frances Hargraves had both a pear and an apple tree on Caldwell Street. Sometimes, we ventured farther—walking south on Broad Street to Carrboro, knocking on doors and asking permission to gather from residents' fruit and nut trees.

At Mr. Morris Mason's home in Carrboro, there were peach, apple, and pear trees, along with a grape arbor. Heading toward Northside Elementary School, we found wild persimmon trees. Eating their fruit before it ripened would pucker and numb our mouths. We soon learned to wait for them to mature and fall from the tree. Once ripe, their soft, orange, wrinkled flesh tasted like candy. The smell of the honeysuckle plant drew us to its tubular yellow and white blooms. After breaking the end of the flower petal and pulling out the white stem, our reward was a tiny drop of nectar full of flavor.

One day, my sister Lane and I discovered a new fruit. We had walked to the playground at Northside Elementary School and were resting under a canopy of trees surrounded by big rocks and boulders arranged in a way that we thought resembled a sitting room. From this vantage point, we spotted a tree with large leaves, heavy with bell-shaped fruit, in Mr. and Mrs. Suggs' backyard. We knocked on their front door, and Mrs. Suggs introduced us to her fig tree. We were amazed by this newfound fruit, which was foreign to us. I picked one up from the ground, quickly wiped it on the hem of my shirt, and bit into its firm outer skin that gave way to a soft center and sweet honey taste, crunchy seeds spreading throughout my mouth with each bite. After eating a few figs, we knew we had found something new to share with the other kids, and we added figs to our foraging map, returning each summer to our generous neighbors' tree.

We faced many challenges as we gathered each fruit and nut in season, picking and eating until we got our fill. The black walnuts were particularly problematic. We did not want to deal with their hard green shells, which turned black over time, and we had difficulty keeping pace with the plentiful fallen nuts. We had to dodge the ones dropping from the tree as we walked beneath the limbs that stretched over the sidewalk and street. The first sign was the rustling of leaves, followed by the sudden thump of a nut hitting a limb before plummeting to the ground.

The flavor rewards were worth having our hands stained purple from the mulberries. We experienced rain falling from dark clouds while the sun was still shining, pain from being stuck in a briar patch, beestings, our clothes covered in prickly cocklebur, and wet shoes and socks from accidental steps into the creek caused by slippery rocks protruding from the water.

We loved those summer days, playing and gathering. But then, a beautiful full moon with an orange glow—like it had touched the earth—appeared, giving extra light to farmers. It was the harvest moon—a reminder that our summer foraging season was coming to an end, and it was time for us to gather the final fruits.

Our favorite plum tree, located at Northside Elementary School, stood at the edge of a wooded area near a flowing stream where we often played. It was big and tall, and surrounded by bushes, some of which had thorns. We would go each day to harvest the ripe plums. We had picked or shaken every last plum from that tree but one. It was big, plump, and purple-red, dripping with dew in the morning and glistening in the sunlight. But there was one problem: It was too high for us to reach. So we gave up on trying to climb up to retrieve it, and hoped someone would find it when it had dropped from the branch.

One day, that plum came to mind—and I was determined to get it. So I took a solo trip to the tree to get that prize plum. I climbed that tree to the top, hugging the trunk with one arm and stretching out my other arm as far as I could reach. As soon as I grabbed the plum, I fell backward and landed on a soft bed of bushes. The first thing I did was open my hand to see if my plum was okay. It was! I walked home, eating that plum with its sweet juice running down my wrist, and showed the seed as proof to the other kids in the neighborhood that I had finally gotten it.

The harvest moon reminds me of the last pick from that plum tree, and picking that plum taught me that if I believed I could do something, I would. I have learned much from being close to the earth, and I now appreciate the end of the harvest because that is when I learned this valuable life lesson.

PLUM AND NECTARINE YOGURT BOWL

WITH WILDFLOWER HONEY GRANOLA

I like to serve this dish family style in a large, shallow bowl—the plums and nectarines resting on the yogurt and topped with homemade granola makes for an inviting presentation. The light, fruity, and rich fragrance of the wildflower honey granola with its delicate crunch will arouse your senses. I like to use Siggi's brand of yogurt because of its thick texture that holds up well with the juices from the fresh fruits. I always make a generous quantity of granola to have on hand, for later.

SERVES 6

FOR THE GRANOLA

3 cups rolled oats
½ cup chopped pecans
1 cup sunflower seeds
½ cup chopped walnuts
⅓ cup wildflower honey
¼ cup brown sugar, packed
¼ cup canola oil

FOR THE YOGURT

1 (24-ounce) container plain yogurt
¼ teaspoon ground cinnamon
6 ripe red plums, pitted and sliced
6 nectarines, pitted and sliced

TO MAKE THE GRANOLA

Preheat the oven to 350°F.

Toss the oats, pecans, sunflower seeds, and walnuts together in a large bowl.

In a small saucepan, combine the honey, brown sugar, and oil. Cook and stir over medium heat until the brown sugar is dissolved and the mixture is bubbly. Pour the honey mixture over the oat mixture and stir until all the oats and nuts are coated. Pour the mixture onto a sheet pan and spread it out in an even layer.

Bake for 18 to 20 minutes, tossing after 10 minutes with a large spatula. Continue baking until golden brown. Remove from the oven and let the granola cool to room temperature. Store in an airtight container.

TO MAKE THE YOGURT BOWL

In a medium bowl, whip together the yogurt and cinnamon. Spoon the yogurt mixture into a serving bowl. Arrange the plums and nectarines over the yogurt. Sprinkle it with granola.

SNACKS AND STARTERS

FRIED CHICKEN LOLLIPOPS

WITH ANDALOUSE SAUCE

Chicken drumettes are transformed into "lollipops" for your next cocktail party. They are exceptional when paired with a tangy homemade andalouse sauce, a Belgian specialty. Prepping the chicken drumettes is time consuming but well worth the effort. Preparing them the day before cooking makes the process much easier.

SERVES 6 TO 8

FOR THE LOLLIPOPS

16 chicken drumettes
2 cups cold water
1½ teaspoons salt
Vegetable oil for frying
2½ cups self-rising flour
½ teaspoon freshly ground black pepper

FOR THE ANDALOUSE SAUCE

1 cup mayonnaise
2 tablespoons roasted red pepper purée
1 tablespoon tomato paste
1 teaspoon white wine vinegar
¼ teaspoon cayenne pepper

TO MAKE THE LOLLIPOPS

Beginning at the narrower end of the chicken drumettes, cut the skin and tendons and scrape the meat toward the thicker end to make a plump drumstick (lollipop) with the bone exposed.

Prepare the brine. In a large bowl, combine the cold water, 1 teaspoon of the salt, and ice. Place the chicken lollipops in the brine, cover, and refrigerate for 1 hour or overnight.

Combine the flour, pepper, and the remaining ½ teaspoon of salt in a medium bowl.

Heat the oil to 325°F. Working in batches, remove 6 lollipops from the brine, letting excess water drip off the pieces. Coat each drumette with the flour mixture. Shake off any excess flour and fry the drumettes for 8 to 10 minutes, or until they are done and golden brown. Drain them on paper towels. Continue coating and frying the drumettes until all are cooked.

TO MAKE THE ANDALOUSE SAUCE

Combine all the ingredients in a medium bowl and whisk until combined.

TO ASSEMBLE

Place the drumettes on a serving platter and drizzle the meaty portion with the andalouse sauce or serve the sauce on the side.

SWEET POTATO CORN BREAD

The sweet potato adds a moist and tender texture along with a natural sweetness to traditional corn bread. Eat the corn bread on its own or sliced and filled with thinly sliced Southern dry-cured country ham or Italian paper-thin prosciutto. Each bite offers a delicious harmony of sweet and savory. This simple pairing transforms comforting sweet potato corn bread into a satisfying handheld snack. The choice is yours: Southern tradition or Italian tradition.

SERVES 6

1 cup all-purpose flour
½ cup cornmeal
¼ cup sugar
1 teaspoon baking powder
½ teaspoon baking soda
½ teaspoon salt
1 teaspoon cinnamon
¼ teaspoon nutmeg
4 tablespoons unsalted butter, chilled
2 eggs, beaten
1 cup mashed, roasted sweet potatoes (about 1 large)
1 tablespoon finely grated orange zest
½ cup buttermilk

Preheat the oven to 350°F.

Grease an 8-by-8-inch baking pan. In a large bowl, stir together the flour, cornmeal, sugar, baking powder, baking soda, salt, cinnamon, and nutmeg. Using a pastry cutter or your fingertips, cut the butter into the flour mixture.

In a separate medium bowl, mix together the eggs, sweet potatoes, orange zest, and buttermilk. Add the egg mixture to the flour mixture and stir together until combined.

Pour the batter into the prepared baking pan and bake for 25 to 30 minutes, until golden brown and the point of a knife inserted into the center comes out clean.

THRIFT SHOPPING

I HAVE AN UNQUENCHABLE thirst for shopping at thrift stores and estate sales. The explanation for my liking comes in five words: conversation, distraction, satisfaction, recreation, and curation. What do these five words have to do with shopping? Let me explain: Conversation comes from my interactions with staff and other frequent shoppers; distraction comes from forgetting about my sometimes hectic life; satisfaction comes from restoring and being creative with my discoveries; recreation comes from enjoying the hunt for that surprising ornament; and curation is both how I look to the past when collecting my objects and how I present them in my space.

My friends often ask me how I always find the finer things. For me, it's about the whole experience. It's knowing what to look for. Remembering the interior decorations of African American women in my community, their aesthetic spaces travel with me across time and influence my thoughts and the need to create that same relaxing atmosphere in my home and to set a beautiful tablescape. I also learned how to recognize quality during my years at Chapel Hill High School. I could be found in the glass-enclosed magazine area of the library, looking at luxury lifestyle magazines. This is where I learned how to identify the good stuff and how to be creative with table settings. I would study the photos and read their captions. I paid close attention to the way the centerpieces were positioned, the designs on the china, the colors of the napkins, and the sparkle on the crystal reflecting from the candlelight. I played a guessing game with myself about how many courses would be served based on the number and position of the silverware laid at each place setting.

I have been told by a few of my siblings that I frequent the thrift shops too often, but after they inspect my treasure trove, they find value in my weekly journey, and they hand me their wish lists to take along on my next trip.

SPICED COCKTAIL PEANUTS

Mama would often take us to the country to help her pick vegetables from the garden she shared with Uncle Wilson. There was a never-ending supply of string beans, corn, sweet potatoes, field peas, okra, watermelon, and cucumbers. Sometimes, Uncle Wilson would pick me up for a solo trip to the garden. He wanted to share his love for the outdoors and the rewards of planting and harvesting with me. One of my favorite things we did together was dig up the sweet potatoes after he used his tractor to loosen the soil. He always had peanuts in his pocket in case we needed a snack while working in the garden. The sunsets over the fields, the crumbling feel of dry soil, and the rich smell of wet earth are the memories I took away from spending time in my family's country garden. I dedicate this recipe to my Uncle Wilson, who was known for his love of all things peanuts.

SERVES 8

- 2 teaspoons red curry powder
- 2 teaspoons sugar
- 1 teaspoon onion powder
- 1 teaspoon granulated garlic
- 1 teaspoon salt
- ½ teaspoon freshly ground black pepper
- 2 teaspoons olive oil
- 2 cups unsalted peanuts

In a small bowl, combine the first six ingredients. Heat the oil in a medium skillet over medium-low heat. Add the spice mixture and stir for a few seconds until the spices are fragrant. Add the peanuts and cook, stirring until the peanuts are coated with the spice mixture and heated through, about 1 minute. Cool completely. Store in an airtight container.

Cheddar Cheese Relish

I was in Texas, in a showroom at the Dallas Market Center, when I noticed a grandmotherly lady preparing a variety of dishes for the trade show attendants to eat. Watching her set up the buffet, I recognized her passion and appreciation for what she was preparing. Not able to identify the cheese dish, I tasted it and tasted it, and did my best to figure it out. This recipe is the dish that my taste buds remembered. I like to serve this relish stuffed in mini phyllo pastry shells or in a small bowl with crackers.

SERVES 8 TO 10

- 2 cups shredded mild cheddar cheese
- ½ cup chopped pecans
- ½ cup crispy bacon, crumbled
- 2 tablespoons chopped fresh Italian parsley
- 1 tablespoon white wine vinegar
- 2 tablespoons olive oil
- ½ teaspoon freshly ground black pepper
- Store-bought mini phyllo pastry shells or crackers

Toss together the first four ingredients in a large bowl. Whisk together the vinegar, olive oil, and pepper. Toss together with the cheese mixture. Serve stuffed in mini phyllo pastry shells or with crackers.

BLT CRACKERS

I found a recipe for bacon-wrapped crackers in the 1985 cookbook *Bluegrass Winners*. I added lettuce and tomato to that recipe to create this version of BLT crackers.

SERVES 6 TO 8

- 6 slices thin bacon
- 16 saltine crackers
- 1 cup iceberg lettuce, finely chopped
- 1 small tomato, seeded and diced
- 2 teaspoons mayonnaise

Preheat the oven to 375°F.

Cut each slice of bacon horizontally into three equal slices. Wrap each piece around a saltine cracker. Place them cut side down on a shallow baking pan, 1 inch apart. Bake for 20 to 25 minutes, or until the bacon is crisp. Remove the bacon-wrapped crackers from the oven, place them on paper towels, and pat off any excess fat.

Toss together the lettuce and tomato in a small bowl, then fold in the mayonnaise.

Place a small spoonful of the lettuce mixture on top of each bacon-wrapped cracker, or serve the lettuce mixture on the side in a small bowl.

HAM TERRINE WITH RITZ CRACKERS

Potted meat is a British dish that came my way in a small tin can at my neighborhood corner store. I loved the sweet and salty flavors of ham and the taste of the spices. We always ate it with Ritz crackers. This terrine will keep in the refrigerator for up to one week.

SERVES 8

- 1 cup (2 sticks) unsalted butter
- 1 pound baked ham
- 1 tablespoon apple cider vinegar
- ¼ teaspoon Dijon mustard
- 1 teaspoon freshly ground black pepper
- ½ teaspoon cinnamon
- ½ teaspoon ground cloves
- Ritz crackers

In a small saucepan over low heat, melt the butter. Remove the butter from the heat and let it settle for 5 minutes. Skim the foam off the top of the butter and discard it. Slowly pour the clear yellow liquid into a bowl. Discard any solids that may have settled to the bottom of the pan. The butter is now clarified.

Place the ham, vinegar, mustard, pepper, cinnamon, cloves, and 2 tablespoons of the clarified butter into a food processor and process until smooth. Divide the mixture into eight small ramekins. Press down with a small spoon or spatula to smooth the surface of the ham. Spoon the remaining clarified butter equally over the top of each dish to cover the ham. Leave the ramekins on the counter until the butter begins to solidify. Cover with plastic wrap, place in the refrigerator, and chill for at least 1 hour, or until the butter is solid.

When you are ready to serve the dish, remove the ramekins from the refrigerator and let them come to room temperature. Serve with Ritz crackers.

HOT CRAB DIP

This dish is inspired by the hot crab casserole I first tasted from a smorgasbord of delicious Outer Banks specialties at River Forest Manor in Belhaven, North Carolina.

SERVES 6

- 2 (8-ounce) packages cream cheese, softened
- ½ cup mayonnaise
- 1 teaspoon lemon juice
- 1 tablespoon lemon zest, finely grated
- ¼ cup Italian parsley, finely chopped
- ¼ teaspoon freshly ground white pepper
- 8 ounces fresh lump crabmeat
- Buttered baguette slices, Ritz crackers, or kettle chips for serving

Preheat the oven to 350°F.

In a mixing bowl, beat together the cream cheese, mayonnaise, and lemon juice until smooth.

Stir in the lemon zest, parsley, and pepper. Gently check to make sure there are no shell pieces in the crabmeat. Fold the crabmeat into the cream cheese mixture. Spoon into a 1-quart baking dish.

Place in the oven and cook for 55 to 60 minutes, or until bubbly and golden brown. Serve with buttered and toasted baguette slices, Ritz crackers, kettle chips, or a combination of all three.

SARDINE AND CREAM CHEESE SPREAD

As a child, after a swim at Hargraves Community Swimming Pool, hunger pangs would hit my stomach, and I would go next door to the snack shack, which was connected to the pool house. One of the snacks I would purchase was sardines and saltine crackers. I seasoned the sardines with cider vinegar, then ate them with the crackers. My grown-up version takes the sardines out of the can and puts them in a bowl with other ingredients, creating layers of sweet and salty flavors.

SERVES 8

- 2 (3¼-ounce) cans boneless and skinless sardines
- 2 tablespoons apple cider vinegar
- 2 (8-ounce) packages cream cheese, softened
- 1 garlic clove, finely minced
- 3 tablespoons red onion, minced
- ⅔ cup golden raisins
- 1 teaspoon fennel seeds
- Saltine crackers

Open and drain the liquid from the sardines. Add 3 teaspoons of the apple cider vinegar to the sardines in each can and let marinate for 15 minutes. Place the sardines in a small bowl and mash them with the back of a fork.

Place the cream cheese in a medium bowl and stir until smooth. Fold the sardines, garlic, onion, raisins, and fennel seeds into the cream cheese. Chill for at least 2 hours before serving. Serve with saltine crackers.

FRESH OKRA FRITTERS

Even though we did not always have baked bread in the house, there was always a canister filled with cornmeal. As a standby, cornmeal and water were mixed together to achieve a thin batter, then fried in lard. Mama always served a platter when we ate fresh fried fish for Friday dinner. I added okra to the basic recipe. These fritters go well with seafood or as a cocktail snack.

NOTE: The batter should be thin enough to spread once it is spooned onto the skillet. If the batter thickens before you fry the batches, add a little water to thin it.

SERVES 6

- 1¼ cups cornmeal
- ½ cup water, more if needed
- 5 to 6 okra pods, stemmed and thinly sliced (about ½ cup fresh okra)
- Vegetable oil for frying
- Coarse sea salt, to taste

In a medium bowl, mix together the cornmeal and water until the mixture is smooth. Stir in the okra.

Pour about ½ inch of vegetable oil into a large skillet. Heat the oil over medium heat to about 325°F. Once the oil is heated, drop the batter by tablespoonfuls into the skillet in batches. Fry each side until crispy and golden brown, about 1 minute on each side. Drain on paper towels. Sprinkle the fritters with coarse sea salt.

HAM-STUFFED EGGS

Black Forest ham really adds flavor to this recipe. Serve these stuffed eggs along with traditional deviled eggs to add variety to your party table.

SERVES 6

- 6 extra large eggs, hard-boiled
- ¼ cup mayonnaise
- ¼ teaspoon yellow mustard
- 2 tablespoons sweet pickle relish
- ¼ cup Black Forest ham, minced

Cut the eggs in half lengthwise, remove the yolks, and place them in a medium bowl, and set the whites aside.

Using a fork, mash together the yolks, mayonnaise, and mustard. Stir until the mixture is smooth. Add the relish and ham and stir well to combine.

Fill the egg white halves with the ham mixture and refrigerate for at least 2 hours.

SOUPS AND SALADS

CREAM OF ASPARAGUS SOUP

WITH MUSHROOM RAGÙ

The meaty flavor of the mushroom ragù elevates the sweet, earthy flavors of the creamy asparagus soup to a new level. The fresh herb garnish adds a boost of fresh flavors, just when you think you have tasted it all.

SERVES 4 TO 6

FOR THE SOUP

1 pound asparagus, trimmed

3 tablespoons unsalted butter

1 garlic clove, minced

½ teaspoon salt

1 quart chicken broth

½ cup half-and-half

2 teaspoons finely grated lemon zest

2 tablespoons chopped fresh thyme

1 tablespoon chopped fresh Italian parsley

1 tablespoon chopped chives

Mushroom Ragù (recipe follows)

FOR THE MUSHROOM RAGÙ

1 tablespoon unsalted butter

2 teaspoons olive oil

1 garlic clove, finely chopped

1 shallot, finely chopped

¼ teaspoon salt

1 (3½-ounce) package shiitake mushrooms, cleaned and coarsely chopped

1 (8-ounce) package cremini mushrooms, cleaned and coarsely chopped

¼ cup dry white wine

TO MAKE THE SOUP

Wash the asparagus and cut it into small pieces.

Melt the butter in a stockpot over medium heat. Add the asparagus, garlic, and salt and cook until fragrant, stirring occasionally. Add the chicken broth and simmer until the asparagus is tender but still green, 10 to 15 minutes. Allow to cool slightly.

Purée the soup in a food processor or blender. Return the soup to the pot. Add the half-and-half and lemon zest and bring the soup back to a simmer. Combine the thyme, parsley, and chives in a small bowl.

TO MAKE THE MUSHROOM RAGÙ

Melt the butter with the olive oil in a medium skillet over medium-low heat. Add the garlic, shallot, salt, and mushrooms. Cook, stirring occasionally, until the mushrooms begin to soften, about 5 minutes. Add the wine and simmer over medium-high heat until the liquid is reduced but not dry—about 5 minutes.

TO ASSEMBLE

Spoon the mushroom ragù into the bottom of individual soup bowls or cups. Ladle the soup into each bowl and garnish with the fresh herbs.

A DATE WITH A DISH

I'VE ALWAYS HAD A fondness for cookbooks—not just for the chance to discover an unusual recipe, but for the stories behind them. I seek out historical cookbooks so I can re-create something new from something traditional. At local thrift shops, I've discovered regional cookbooks from Southern states and beyond. Included in my collection are cookbooks from South Carolina, Alabama, Georgia, Florida, Louisiana, Kentucky, Virginia, Texas, Tennessee, Maryland, Maine, and even other countries, such as Italy, Mexico, and France. These books not only give me insight into what folks in Chapel Hill and Carrboro were once reading and cooking, but they also hint at where those original owners may have traveled or even lived.

One treasured find is a copy of *I Hear America Cooking*—a book that once belonged to Mrs. Edith Murphy, a daily diner at Mama Dip's Kitchen who became a family friend. When I opened it, I was surprised and delighted to see her name inscribed on the front endpaper: "For Edith Murphy, a wonderful cook, Betty Fussell." I cherish that book because of its connection to Mrs. Murphy.

A non-regional book that has particularly inspired me is *A Date with a Dish: A Cookbook of American Negro Recipes* by Freda De Knight, published in 1948. Originally the title of her monthly column in *Ebony* magazine, the book introduced readers to African American caterers, bakers, chefs, cooks, candymakers, and homemakers she met on her travels—each offering their own recipes and a "date" with a dish. The title sparked my own idea of having a date with a dish, drawing on the elements of taste—sweet, sour, salty, peppery, bitter, spicy, tangy, herbal, and mouthfeel—in order to re-create the recipes.

Sometimes, I encounter a dish at a restaurant or event that piques my interest so much that I give it a slow taste, identifying its flavors and ingredients, developing the recipe in my mind. Then, back in my kitchen, I have a date with that dish, re-creating it from memory. These experiences inspire me to bring those flavors into my own repertoire, whether it's a surprising Cheddar Cheese Relish (page 58), which I first encountered at a trade show in Dallas; a unique Grape and Walnut Salad (page 79) from a Sunday brunch buffet at Hotel Europa in Chapel Hill; or the Chilled Cucumber Soup (page 74) at a wedding brunch at Orient Express, an upscale restaurant in Carrboro. Because I was able to re-create these recipes from taste, I can continue to enjoy eating them and also introduce them to guests at my own table.

I also have dates with a dish when I reimagine recipes, adding new components—like adding herbs, garlic, and olive oil to a salmon recipe with pecans that a friend had been served and wanted me to make for her, or pairing Mama's signature salad dressing with a new twist on Iceberg Wedges with Cucumbers and Black Forest Ham (page 80). I even transformed a community cookbook's bacon-wrapped cracker into my own version, calling it BLT Crackers (page 61), by adding mayonnaise, lettuce, and tomato.

What is *your* date with a dish?

Chilled Cucumber Soup
WITH SMOKED SALMON

My first taste of chilled cucumber soup came at the Orient Express restaurant in Carrboro, an upscale dining venue housed in vintage train cars near Carr Mill Mall. The chef there was one of Mama Dip's regular customers. The refreshing taste of chilled cucumber soup is the perfect backdrop to salty, smoky salmon. Add this delightful soup to your lunch or dinner menu or serve it in petite cups as a pleasing addition to afternoon tea.

SERVES 4

3 medium cucumbers, peeled, seeded, and diced
1 cup sour cream
1 tablespoon grated red onion
1 teaspoon salt
1 teaspoon freshly ground black pepper
1 (4-ounce) package smoked salmon, diced

Place the cucumbers, sour cream, red onion, salt, and pepper in a blender or food processor fitted with a metal blade and process until smooth. Pour the mixture into a large bowl. Cover and refrigerate until thoroughly chilled.

Ladle the soup into bowls and place 1 tablespoon of salmon in the center of each serving.

Cream of Turnip Soup
WITH CRISPY GREENS

Although any turnips will do, young turnips give this soup an especially delicate and slightly sweet flavor. The poppy seeds add a nutty aroma and appealing appearance. As the crispy turnip greens meet the soup, they create a symphony of textures—initially crunchy, then gradually softening.

SERVES 4 TO 6

- 2 pounds baby turnips with greens still attached
- 4 tablespoons unsalted butter
- 3 cups chicken broth
- ¼ cup heavy cream
- 1 teaspoon salt
- ½ teaspoon poppy seeds
- ¼ cup olive oil

Remove the greens from the turnips. Rinse the greens under cold running water and dry them thoroughly. Stack the greens, roll them up into a tight bundle, slice them very thinly, then set them aside. Peel and dice the turnips.

Melt the butter in a medium pot over medium heat. Stir in the turnips and cook them for 5 minutes. Add the chicken broth and simmer for 15 to 20 minutes, or until the turnips are tender. Cool slightly.

Pour the soup into a blender or food processor fitted with a metal blade and process until smooth. Return the soup to the pot and stir in the cream and salt. Simmer until the soup is hot. Stir in the poppy seeds.

Preheat the oven to 400°F. Place the turnip greens in a mixing bowl and drizzle with the olive oil. Toss together, coating the greens evenly with the oil. Line the bottom of a baking pan with parchment paper. Spread out the prepared turnip greens evenly on the pan. Roast the turnip greens in the oven for 5 minutes. Flip them over and continue roasting for 5 minutes, or until crispy. Ladle the soup into bowls and garnish each serving with the crispy greens.

BEET, APRICOT, AND GOAT CHEESE SALAD

Select small to medium beets, as these will be more tender and flavorful. The walnut oil vinaigrette lets the flavors of the beets and apricots shine, marries well with the beet juice, and gives the salad a mosaic-like color that looks beautiful on a plate when topped with crumbled goat cheese.

SERVES 8

- 1 cup dried apricots
- 2 pounds fresh beets, green tops removed, leaving a 1-inch length of stem
- ½ cup walnut oil
- ¼ cup apple cider vinegar
- ¼ teaspoon Dijon mustard
- ½ teaspoon salt
- ½ teaspoon sugar
- 1 (3-ounce) package goat cheese

In a small saucepan, bring water to a simmer and poach the apricots for 10 minutes. Remove the apricots from the water with a slotted spoon and cut each one in half.

Put the beets in a large pot and add enough water to cover them by 1 inch. Bring the water to a boil and cook the beets until the point of a knife inserts easily, 20 to 30 minutes. Peel the beets by running cold water over them while scraping them with a knife. Cut the beets into quarters lengthwise.

In a bowl, combine the walnut oil, apple cider vinegar, Dijon mustard, salt, and sugar. Place the beets, apricots, and vinaigrette in a medium bowl and toss them together. When you are ready to serve the salad, place it on a serving dish and crumble the goat cheese over the top.

WATERMELON SALAD

I like to prep each component of the salad and toss them together just before serving. Doing so keeps the salad dressing from becoming diluted from the juice of the watermelon.

SERVES 8

- 3 tablespoons fresh lemon juice
- ½ cup extra-virgin olive oil
- ½ teaspoon salt
- 1 medium seedless watermelon (about 6 cups), chilled
- 1 pound grape tomatoes
- 1 small red onion, diced
- 1 pound arugula
- ½ pound feta cheese, crumbled

Whisk together the lemon juice, olive oil, and salt. Store in a covered jar. Cut the watermelon in half lengthwise and cut out the flesh from both halves with a melon scoop or cut into bite-size cubes and place in a large bowl. Cover and refrigerate. Cut the tomatoes in half lengthwise, place in a bowl, cover, and refrigerate. Soak the red onion in iced water for 15 minutes. Drain the onion, pat dry, and place in a small bowl. Cover and refrigerate.

Just before serving, gently toss together the watermelon, tomatoes, onion, and arugula. Shake the vinaigrette dressing to recombine, add to the salad, and gently toss to coat. Place the watermelon salad in a large bowl and sprinkle with feta cheese.

GRAPE AND WALNUT SALAD

I first ate this salad at Hotel Europa in Chapel Hill—a favorite spot to brunch and lunch with my friends. Walnuts are a perfect match for this crisp, creamy grape salad. They give it a rich, buttery flavor. It rests well on a bed of arugula, which counteracts the sweetness of the grapes, and brings up the nuttiness of the walnuts.

SERVES 8

- 2 pounds seedless grapes
- 1½ cups walnuts, chopped
- 4 ounces cream cheese
- 2 tablespoons sour cream
- 2 tablespoons brown sugar
- 1 teaspoon fresh lemon juice
- 1 tablespoon grated lemon zest

Preheat the oven to 350°F.

Remove the grapes from the stems, then wash and dry them on paper towels. Spread the walnuts on a cookie sheet in one layer and toast them in the preheated oven for 5 to 7 minutes, until they are golden brown with a toasty aroma.

Beat together the cream cheese, sour cream, brown sugar, and lemon juice in a medium bowl until the sugar dissolves. Stir in the lemon zest. Toss the walnuts and grapes together in a large bowl. Add the cream mixture and stir to combine.

ICEBERG WEDGES

WITH CUCUMBERS AND BLACK FOREST HAM

The crispiness of iceberg lettuce pairs well with the mild and salty flavors of Black Forest ham and the slightly sweet taste of the salad dressing. I sometimes add grape tomatoes, sliced in half, for a pop of color.

SERVES 6

2 heads iceberg lettuce
1 cup mayonnaise
2 teaspoons Dijon mustard
2 tablespoons apple cider vinegar
½ teaspoon salt
2 small cucumbers, seeded and diced
¼ pound thick-cut Black Forest ham, diced
1 pint grape tomatoes, sliced in half lengthwise (optional)

Cut the lettuce heads into 6 wedges. Rinse them under cold running water, then shake the water from the lettuce, making sure the wedges stay intact. Wrap them in paper towels. Refrigerate them until you are ready to use them.

In a bowl, whisk together the mayonnaise, Dijon mustard, vinegar, and salt. Cover and refrigerate the dressing for at least 2 hours to chill it.

Place the lettuce wedges on individual plates or on a large platter. Sprinkle the wedges with the cucumber, ham, and tomatoes (if using). Drizzle the salad dressing on top.

Caesar Salad

WITH ARUGULA AND GARLIC CROUTONS

I added arugula leaves to my Caesar salad at a salad bar one day and discovered that the peppery and nutty flavors of the arugula complemented the mild flavor and crunchy texture of the romaine lettuce.

SERVES 6

FOR THE SALAD

- 2 tablespoons unsalted butter, melted
- 1 garlic clove, crushed
- 3 cups French bread, cubed
- 2 heads romaine lettuce, cut into bite-size pieces
- 4 cups baby arugula
- 3 tablespoons grated Parmesan cheese

FOR THE DRESSING

- 1 cup mayonnaise
- ½ cup heavy cream
- 2 teaspoons Dijon mustard
- 2 anchovy fillets, mashed
- 1 teaspoon fresh lemon juice
- 1 teaspoon freshly ground black pepper
- 1 tablespoon grated Parmesan cheese

TO MAKE THE SALAD

Preheat the oven to 325°F.

Combine the melted butter with the garlic and toss them with the bread cubes. Arrange the cubes on a baking sheet in a single layer. Bake until the croutons are golden brown and crispy, about 10 minutes. In a large bowl, toss together the romaine, arugula, croutons, and Parmesan cheese.

TO MAKE THE DRESSING

In a small bowl, whisk together the mayonnaise, heavy cream, Dijon mustard, anchovies, lemon juice, black pepper, and Parmesan cheese.

TO ASSEMBLE

When ready to serve, drizzle the salad with a few tablespoons (or more) of Caesar dressing and toss until the lettuce is evenly coated.

STRAWBERRY, ROMAINE, AND RED ONION SALAD

At one of my dinner parties, I served this salad as the French do, after the main course and before the cheese course or dessert, to cleanse the palate. I can tell you from experience, it works.

SERVES 6

2 cups strawberries
1 large head of romaine lettuce
1 small red onion, sliced thin
½ cup olive oil
2 tablespoons white wine vinegar
2 tablespoons honey
1 teaspoon Dijon mustard
½ teaspoon salt

Wash, hull, and dice the strawberries. Wash, dry, and cut the lettuce into julienne strips. Soak the onion slices in iced water for 10 minutes, then drain them and pat dry. Toss the strawberries, lettuce, and onion together in a large bowl.

Whisk the olive oil, vinegar, honey, Dijon mustard, and salt together in a small bowl. Pour the dressing over the salad and toss gently until well combined.

ASPARAGUS AND SWEET PEPPER SALAD

I first prepared this salad for my niece's birthday party, and it was a hit. Piquillo, a sweet pepper from Spain, adds a nice tangy flavor. I like to make this salad the same day I am going to serve it so that it retains the crunchiness and bright green color of the asparagus.

SERVES 8

2 pounds medium asparagus, trimmed

½ teaspoon salt, plus more for the water

1 cup piquillo peppers (jarred), diced

6 tablespoons olive oil

2 tablespoons white wine vinegar

¼ teaspoon white pepper

2 tablespoons chopped fresh Italian parsley

2 teaspoons finely grated lemon zest

Cook the asparagus in a large skillet filled with boiling salted water until it is tender, 3 to 4 minutes. Drain well. Place the asparagus in a shallow dish and toss it together with the peppers.

Whisk together the olive oil, vinegar, salt, and white pepper in a small bowl. Pour the dressing over the asparagus. Toss together. Sprinkle the parsley and lemon zest over the top. Serve at room temperature.

VEGETABLE SIDES

HEART OF THE HOME

OUR HOME'S MOST UTILIZED piece of furniture, and our social center, was the mid-century dining table in the middle of our kitchen. This was where my siblings and I ate, played board and card games, did our homework, and talked about our daily activities. It had a white feathery-patterned top and a shiny, slick surface. Whenever we placed an iced beverage glass on the table, condensation would cause the glass to slide until it reached the slightly raised edge. The matching curved, chrome-legged chairs had vinyl seats in the same pattern as the tabletop.

Mama had instructed us to leave the table only when we had eaten everything on our plates. We laughed together as we tried to swallow the last morsel of food when Mama served something we didn't like. One of my siblings had learned in school that the nose plays an essential role in taste, and taught us how to get through our meals without the unpleasant flavors by manipulating our olfactory system. We would pinch our nostrils together, stopping the odor from getting to the back of our noses as we chewed and swallowed.

This memory brings to mind the lima bean, a cute, light green, kidney-shaped legume that most of my siblings (including me) disliked because of its starchy taste. We even had to harvest them from Mama's country garden, shelling them by pulling the string along the seam of the pod, splitting it open with our fingers, then releasing the seeds into a bowl. When lima beans showed up in our meals, we would simultaneously pinch our noses together, making sure our mouths were not open while chewing, to clear those lima beans from our plates. We would laugh at whoever had the most food left that they disliked.

I still don't care for lima beans, but they were always one of the most popular legumes at Mama Dip's Kitchen.

BRAISED COLLARD GREENS

Mama had a way with vegetables and taught us to cook them in true Southern style. Watching her prepare greens, we learned the subtle difference between how she cooked turnip greens and collard greens, which was due to the use of fatback. For turnip greens, Mama boiled the fatback until it flavored the water, then added the fresh greens and simmered them until tender. With collard greens, she fried the fatback first to render its fat, then added it to the greens after draining most of the "pot liquor." Whether she was preparing collard or turnip greens, she always took a bite to test their tenderness.

At our Southern table, collard greens are always served with raw onions and pepper vinegar. This recipe builds the seasonings right into the cooking process, adding a little spicy heat from the jalapeños. You can reserve the rendered fatback as a snack, or serve it alongside as a condiment.

SERVES 6

2 (¾- to 1-pound bunches) collard greens
1 teaspoon salt, plus more to taste
1 tablespoon olive oil
4 slices fatback
2 medium onions, chopped
2 garlic cloves, diced
¼ cup diced jalapeño peppers
2 tablespoons apple cider vinegar

Wash the collard greens thoroughly in cold water. Remove the stems and cut the collards into bite-size pieces. Place the collards and salt in a large pot. Pour in enough water to cover the collards by 2 inches. Bring the water to a boil. Simmer for 30 to 45 minutes, or until the collards are tender.

Add the olive oil to a medium skillet and fry the fatback on both sides, 30 to 40 seconds, over medium-low heat. Remove the fatback from the skillet once it is crispy and golden brown. Add the onions and garlic. Cook until the onions are softened, 8 to 10 minutes. Drain the liquid from the collards. Stir in the onion mixture. Add the jalapeño peppers, vinegar, and salt to taste. Cook for 5 minutes.

STEWED CORN

As children, my siblings and I would gather around Mama in the kitchen to watch her technique as she removed kernels from freshly shucked ears of corn. She guided the knife from the tip of the ear down to the shank, slicing off the kernels before pressing the blade along the cob to remove the "milk." We would anticipate the shower of corn milk that sprinkled our faces. Once she started cooking, the milk thickened the corn as it simmered in a skillet with fat rendered from slices of fatback. She never needed to add much salt, because the pork provided just the right amount of seasoning.

Years later, one of the fashion world's brightest stars, André Leon Talley, would sit at my table and savor this dish. A Durham native who rose to international fame as *Vogue*'s creative director and *Vanity Fair*'s European editor, André never lost his Southern roots. He was a cherished regular at the restaurant—and a friend. Stewed corn, just the way Mama made it, was one of his favorites. He always asked for extra servings—just like family.

To make this dish vegetarian, substitute butter for the fatback, adding two tablespoons at the end of cooking for flavor.

SERVES 6

8 to 10 ears of corn
1 tablespoon all-purpose flour
4 ¼-inch fatback strips
2 cups water
Salt

Shuck and remove the silk from the corn. Cut the corn off the cob, then scrape the cob to render the corn "milk" into a medium bowl. Stir in the flour. Set aside.

Over medium-low heat, place the fatback in a large skillet and fry on both sides until crispy and the fat is rendered, 30 to 40 seconds on each side. Remove the fatback. Add the water to the corn mixture and pour into the skillet with the fat. Cook over medium heat, stirring until the corn is tender, about 10 minutes. Season with salt to taste.

TANGY POTATO SALAD

Southerners traditionally make potato salad with sweet pickle relish. My sister Norma introduced me to this version of Southern potato salad that uses tangy dill pickle relish and sour cream. This salad is a tasty side dish that you can serve with fried chicken and baked ham.

SERVES 8

- 3 pounds potatoes, russet or Idaho
- 1 teaspoon salt, plus more for the pot
- ¼ cup diced red onion
- 1 cup mayonnaise
- 3 hard-boiled eggs, grated
- ½ cup dill pickle relish
- ¼ cup sour cream
- 1 tablespoon finely chopped fresh Italian parsley
- 2 teaspoons mustard

Boil the potatoes in salted water until they are tender, 25 to 30 minutes. Let them cool until you are able to handle them. Soak the red onion in iced water for 5 minutes. Drain and pat dry. Peel the potatoes, cut them into chunks, and place them in a large bowl. Add the onion and remaining ingredients and toss to combine. Chill the salad in the refrigerator for at least 2 hours.

COUNTRY-FRIED CABBAGE

I find the flavors of olive oil mixed with fatback to be pleasing in this country-style cabbage side dish.

SERVES 6

- 2 teaspoons olive oil
- 4 slices fatback, cut ¼ inch thick
- 1 medium cabbage, cored and sliced
- ¼ cup water
- 1 teaspoon crushed red pepper
- ½ teaspoon salt

Over medium-low heat, pour the olive oil into a large saucepan. Add the fatback in a single layer and fry until it is golden brown and crispy, 35 to 40 seconds on each side. Remove the fatback from the pan and drain on paper towels. When the fatback is cool enough to handle, cut the crackling away from the skin (which you can eat as a snack or discard), and dice. Set aside.

Meanwhile, add the cabbage to the saucepan and stir to coat it with the olive oil and drippings from the fatback. Add the water, red pepper, and salt to the cabbage. Cook over medium heat until the cabbage is tender, about 10 minutes. Place the fried cabbage in a serving dish and top it with the crackling.

MACARONI AND CHEESE

I love the combination of creamy cheddar cheese paired with the fruity and nutty flavors of Parmesan, which adds a little extra savoriness to classic macaroni and cheese.

SERVES 8

2 cups elbow macaroni
½ teaspoon salt, plus more for the pot
½ cup (1 stick) unsalted butter
½ cup all-purpose flour
2½ cups milk
1 egg yolk, lightly beaten
¼ teaspoon paprika
4 cups (1 pound) grated mild cheddar cheese
½ cup grated Parmesan cheese

Preheat the oven to 350°F.

Put the macaroni in 3 quarts of boiling salted water. Cook the macaroni until firm, 6 to 8 minutes. Drain well. In a medium saucepan, melt the butter over medium-low heat. Whisk in the flour until the mixture is smooth. Gradually whisk in the milk. Cook for about 5 minutes over medium-low heat until slightly thickened.

In a small bowl, whisk 1 tablespoon of the sauce into the egg yolk. Whisk the egg yolk mixture into the sauce and stir over low heat until thickened, 2 to 3 minutes. Add the paprika, salt, 2 cups of the cheddar cheese, and the Parmesan cheese. Stir until the cheese melts. Combine with the macaroni. Pour the mixture into a 9-by-13 or 3-quart casserole dish and sprinkle the remaining cheddar cheese over the top. Bake for 20 to 25 minutes, or until creamy and bubbly.

APPLE COLESLAW

Adding apples and fresh dill gives classic Southern coleslaw additional layers of flavor, color, and deliciousness.

SERVES 6

- 2 Granny Smith apples
- 1 tablespoon fresh lemon juice
- 4 cups finely shredded cabbage (about 1 small cabbage)
- ½ cup mayonnaise
- 1 tablespoon white wine vinegar
- 1 tablespoon sugar
- ¼ cup chopped fresh dill

Core and dice the apples, then place them in a large bowl and toss with the lemon juice. Add the cabbage and toss together.

Prepare the dressing. Combine the mayonnaise, vinegar, and sugar in a small bowl. Whisk until the sugar dissolves. Add the dressing to the cabbage mixture and toss well. Stir in the dill. Cover and refrigerate the salad for at least 2 hours before serving.

A SENSE OF PLACE

STROLLING THROUGH THE NEIGHBORHOOD during dinnertime, I could tell what was cooking in each home just by the aromas that filled the air. The sweet scent of roasted sweet potatoes came from my paternal grandmother's kitchen—the key to the natural sweetness and caramel flavors of her treasured sweet potato pie recipe for my grandparents' restaurant, Bill's Bar-B-Q. The earthy, fatty aromas coming from a simmering pot of pinto beans wafted from the home of a family that did not have a lot but made the most of what they had with sweet corn bread, fried fatback, and chopped raw onions to complete the meal. As I walked from street to street, aromatic clouds stretched from each kitchen window, vanishing until I came upon the smells of another cook's kitchen. The smell of collard greens fought against the foul scent of chitterlings cooking (a special treat in the South) but found a place in the backdrop of the flavor clouds floating over my nostrils. Cakes baking, chicken frying, and sometimes the whiff of burnt food were part of the scene.

My culinary heritage extends from my mother's kitchen to many others where I was welcomed, fed, and taught. Just as terroir with its natural conditions shapes a wine's unique traits, my food terroir was shaped both by my cultural heritage and a sense of place. It shaped my growth from a curious kid to an adult foodie. During those times spent in their homes, my territory was defined.

Terrain defined the atmosphere of each home, the surroundings, and the sense of belonging that came with each meal. Climate dictated what was on the table according to the season, with ingredients locally sourced from family gardens planted in Chatham County—just 12 miles from our home in

Chapel Hill—or from a community garden in a friend's large, sunny backyard only a few blocks away. I contributed to planting, harvesting, and preparing vegetables, learning our family's historical gardening tradition firsthand from my mother and her siblings. I came to understand that the taste and texture of homegrown fruits and vegetables brought from the farm to the table are the best.

Each cook created their own unique taste, adding their own flavors and textures to recipes that had been handed down orally from generation to generation. In recipes calling for sweet potatoes—sometimes called yams—seasoning choices varied. My grandmother favored cinnamon, while others preferred nutmeg, and some used a combination of both, always adding vanilla. Although they had their favorite flavorings for a dish, they all shared a common approach: They tasted as they added ingredients to achieve the best results. More importantly, they shared their tables, giving advice and wisdom.

I loved visiting the gardens, farms, and kitchens of my community. Today, the flavor clouds released from my own kitchen into my neighborhood show, and are part of, my expanded terroir.

PURPLE HULL PEAS AND CORN

This is one of my all-time favorites that Mama would prepare for our dinner table and at Mama Dip's Kitchen when purple hull peas were in season.

SERVES 8

- 1 smoked ham hock
- 3 cups shelled purple hull peas, about 1 pound
- 1 garlic clove
- 1 teaspoon salt
- 2 cups fresh corn, from about 4 ears

Place the ham hock, purple hull peas, garlic clove, and salt in a large saucepan. Add enough water to cover the ham hock by 2 inches. Bring the water to a boil. Reduce the heat and simmer for 25 to 30 minutes, until the peas are nearly done. Remove the ham hock and discard. Stir in the corn and continue cooking for 7 to 10 minutes, until the peas and corn are tender.

STRING BEANS
WITH FRESH HERBS

The pleasant fragrance of fresh herbs sprinkled over string beans is a lovely combination in this savory and easy-to-prepare side dish.

SERVES 8

- 2 pounds string beans, trimmed
- 2 teaspoons salt
- 2 tablespoons olive oil
- 2 tablespoons butter
- 1 tablespoon fresh lemon juice
- 1 tablespoon chopped fresh basil
- 1 tablespoon chopped fresh Italian parsley

Put the string beans and salt in a large saucepan. Add enough water to cover the string beans. Bring the water to a boil, then reduce heat to a simmer. Cook the string beans until they are tender but not limp. Drain the water. Add the olive oil, butter, and lemon juice to a large skillet. Warm over low heat until the butter melts. Add the string beans, basil, and parsley and toss together.

SPINACH, PARMESAN, AND ARTICHOKE GRATIN

This dish elevates a simple menu of roasted meat or fish, and it is a good choice if you're asked to bring a special dish to a holiday table.

SERVES 6

1 tablespoon olive oil
2 pounds baby spinach, rinsed and drained
½ teaspoon salt
2 (14-ounce) cans artichoke hearts
1 cup heavy cream
½ cup grated Parmesan cheese
1½ cups bread crumbs
3 tablespoons unsalted butter, melted

Preheat the oven to 375°F.

Heat the olive oil in a large skillet over medium heat. Add the spinach and salt to the olive oil and sauté until wilted, 1 to 2 minutes. Drain the spinach, then squeeze out any excess moisture. Transfer the spinach to a shallow 9-by-13 or 3-quart casserole dish and spread evenly. Cut the artichoke hearts lengthwise into halves and arrange them cut side down in a single layer over the spinach. Pour the cream evenly over the top. Sprinkle the Parmesan cheese over the top of the artichokes.

Combine the bread crumbs and melted butter in a small bowl. Sprinkle the buttered bread crumbs over the gratin. Bake until hot and bubbly and the bread crumbs are golden brown, 15 to 20 minutes.

ONION POTATOES

This was one of my father's favorite side dishes. Mama usually served onion potatoes on Fish Friday along with coleslaw.

SERVES 8

6 medium potatoes, about 3 pounds
1 medium onion, chopped
4 tablespoons unsalted butter, melted
1 teaspoon salt
½ teaspoon black pepper

Peel and cut the potatoes into bite-size cubes. Place the potatoes in a large pot and add enough water to cover them by 1 inch. Bring the water to a boil and cook the potatoes until almost tender, 12 to 15 minutes. Add the onion and continue cooking until the potatoes are tender, about 5 minutes. Using a mesh strainer, drain all but 2 tablespoons of the water from the potatoes and place any strained onion back in the pot. Add the butter, salt, and pepper and stir gently to combine.

SWEET POTATO AND APPLE BAKE

For a complete Southern meal, serve this creamy sweet potato and apple dish with Braised Collard Greens (page 90) along with Smothered Fried Chicken with Andouille Sausage (page 116). Your taste buds will be well pleased.

SERVES 6

- ½ cup light brown sugar, packed
- 1 teaspoon ground cinnamon
- 2 medium sweet potatoes
- 2 medium Granny Smith apples
- 2 tablespoons fresh lemon juice
- 4 tablespoons unsalted butter, melted

Preheat the oven to 350°F.

Combine the brown sugar and cinnamon in a small bowl. Set aside. Peel the sweet potatoes and cut them into cubes. Peel and core the apples and cut them into cubes. Toss the apples in the lemon juice. Place the sweet potatoes and apples in a 1-quart baking dish. Add the melted butter and sugar mixture and toss to combine.

Cover with a lid or foil and bake for 30 minutes, stirring once, halfway through. Uncover and continue baking for 20 to 25 minutes, or until the potatoes and apples are tender.

BRÛLÉED CORN PUDDING

This recipe is inspired by the Fresh Corn Casserole recipe from my mother's first cookbook, *Mama Dip's Kitchen.* A burnt sugar coating adds sweetness and gives a French accent to this Southern side dish.

SERVES 6

4 eggs, beaten
2 cups half-and-half
3 cups fresh corn, cut from the cob (about 6 medium ears)
1 tablespoon all-purpose flour
4 tablespoons unsalted butter, melted
1 tablespoon minced fresh chives
1 tablespoon minced fresh basil
½ teaspoon white pepper
⅓ cup light brown sugar, packed

Preheat the oven to 350°F.

Beat the eggs and half-and-half together in a large bowl. Combine the corn, flour, butter, chives, basil, and pepper in a medium bowl. Add the egg mixture and stir together until well mixed. Pour into a 1½-quart casserole dish. Bake for 50 to 60 minutes, or until the point of a knife comes out clean or the custard is set.

Sprinkle the brown sugar evenly over the custard. Use a kitchen torch to melt and brown the sugar or place the custard under a broiler until bubbly and dark brown—20 to 30 seconds.

MAINS

PLUMP DUMPLING ENCOUNTERS

CHICKEN AND DUMPLINGS WAS a dish occasionally served for our Sunday meal and was often taken to annual church homecoming dinners. Hens simmered on the stove until the meat fell off the bones. When the chicken was ready, Mama brought the pot to the dining table so we could help her pull the meat from the bones. Mama instructed us to discard the fat, skin, and veins. Once the broth was strained and clarified, she set aside a portion to make the dumpling dough, and returned the rest to a large pot on the stove. She then added butter to the broth and left it to simmer.

Next, Mama used her hands to scoop the flour into a bowl, pouring chicken broth into the flour a little at a time until her fingers felt the correct texture. When the dough became smooth and felt airy when touched, she handed us a piece to feel. We had seen the stickiness of the dough after she'd added the broth, and now we felt the smooth and light texture that told us it was ready to be rolled.

Dusting the tabletop with flour, she rolled the dough until it was thin. Using a table knife, we helped her cut the rolled dough into squares, and we watched as Mama gently placed her hands over the pieces of dough and then slid them into the pot, where they immediately sank. She returned to add another batch of dough to the pot. I noticed that the noodles had already begun to float on top of the broth. The broth had slightly thickened from the flour that fell from the dough and Mama's hands. As the noodles simmered, we watched their metamorphosis; the noodles had absorbed the broth, thickened slightly, floated lightly, and were moving around in the simmering broth. No longer were they pieces of thin, raw dough.

Finally, Mama added the chicken pieces to the pot. With a large wooden spoon, she stirred the broth to distribute them, added salt to taste, and left the chicken and dumplings to stew gently. She handed each of us a tasting spoon that held an undercooked dumpling. We blew on it before taking a bite. The dumplings were ready when their raw aroma changed to the smell of rich, buttery broth and stewed chicken, and when they floated lightly at the surface of the broth, infused with chicken flavor, and felt airy in the mouth.

Years later, when I moved in to my first apartment, I decided to try my hand at preparing chicken and dumplings. Wanting to get the proportions right for the dumplings, I found a recipe in a Southern cookbook, took it to my mother, and asked if it was good. She said, "Do not use this recipe; find a noodle recipe."

I did not realize it was a recipe for drop dumplings—a biscuit-type dough that had to be formed into balls before being dropped into the broth. "Thank you, Mama," I said. I searched for and found a noodle recipe. I used it to make delicious dumplings, adding fresh tarragon to the recipe to make it my own. I did not need to ask her how to make chicken and dumplings because I vividly remembered her making them during our time spent together in the kitchen.

Some of my encounters with drop dumplings came by way of an insult—and by way of necessity.

It wasn't until years later, while working as a server at Mama Dip's Kitchen that I realized just how passionate people could be about their version of a dish. The insult came from a young woman I was serving one day. She had ordered chicken and dumplings, and I proudly set a steaming bowl of my mother's aromatic version on the table before her. She looked at me fiercely and shouted, "What is this?" Using her fork, she lifted a rolled dumpling to show me, and then slammed it back into the bowl. Then, she shouted, "These are not dumplings! Do you call these dumplings? You must be out of your mind! What is all this chicken? This is not the way to make dumplings! They should be round!" She continued shouting, "Round like the ones my grandmother made!"

Steam puffed out of her nostrils and fire came out of her eyes like an angry cartoon character. A rolled dumpling triggered outrage.

I thought to myself, as I stood at the table in shock, *I am not sure what is happening with her, and I will leave it alone, period.*

Her companion was silent, subtly moving her open hands palms down repeatedly and swaying up and down toward the table to calm her down. It didn't work. She did manage to get her to leave, still visibly and verbally upset while exiting through the dining room and out the door.

I guess you don't mess with folks' heritage.

Later, I found myself wondering where she had grown up, since her grandmother used dropped dumplings for chicken and dumplings. That day, I learned an important lesson: People cook the same dish differently depending on where they're from. I would have loved to talk with her about her grandmother's dumpling recipe, but she had other plans.

Mama taught us to laugh at our mishaps and not take things too seriously. I had to remind myself of that years later when I was invited to present a cooking demonstration at a Friends of the Library event at Wiggins Memorial Library at Campbell University.

I decided to make chicken and dumplings. The evening before the event, I measured everything according to Mama's recipe from her cookbook. I prepared my mise en place (all my needed ingredients), and placed everything—including the flour—in the refrigerator.

The next day, standing in front of the audience, I said "Always add your ingredients a little at a time because sometimes flour may be milled differently and may not require the same measure of liquid as the recipe calls for." Then, I proceeded to add all my broth into the flour mixture.

Then, the worst thing happened.

My dough was too wet. In hindsight, I realized that the flour picked up moisture in the refrigerator.

I quickly turned it into a lesson on improvising and immediately went into rescue mode. "If your dough becomes too soggy," I told the audience, "instead of making the rolled dough, use a spoon and scoop the too-wet dough directly into the broth."

It worked. The dumplings were light, fluffy, and delicious.

I was saved by a quick reminder to always have a backup plan, even if it shows up like a lightning flash. The hours spent in the kitchen with Mama had given me more than just a recipe—they had given me patience and the ability to turn a kitchen mishap into a lesson worth sharing.

CHICKEN AND DROP DUMPLINGS

Through a cooking mishap, I discovered drop dumplings can have two textures: light and fluffy on the outside and tender on the inside. To bolster their flavor, I add fresh tarragon. I remember the first time I made this dish and took it to my mother to try. These are not the dumplings that she cooked, but she loved the taste of my version and gave me her approval. I felt good about my success at my first attempt, leaving me with a big blush of a smile.

SERVES 6

FOR THE CHICKEN

- 1 whole chicken (3¾ to 4 pounds)
- 1 teaspoon salt
- 4 tablespoons unsalted butter
- 2 tablespoons chicken base
- Drop Dumplings (recipe follows)
- 2 tablespoons chopped fresh tarragon

FOR THE DROP DUMPLINGS

- 2 cups all-purpose flour
- 2 teaspoons baking powder
- ½ teaspoon salt
- ¾ cup milk
- 2 tablespoons unsalted butter, melted
- 1 egg, lightly beaten

TO MAKE THE CHICKEN

Wash the chicken and place it in a large pot. Add enough water to cover the chicken. Add the salt and bring to a boil over high heat. Reduce the heat to medium-high and cook until the chicken is done and begins to fall off the bone, about 1 hour. Remove the chicken from the pot and set aside to cool. Remove the meat from the chicken and cut it into bite-size pieces. Set aside. Skim the fat from the top of the chicken broth in the pot. Strain the broth and return it to the pot, adding water to make 10 cups.

Add the butter and chicken base to the broth and simmer over low heat while making the dumplings.

TO MAKE THE DROP DUMPLINGS

In a large mixing bowl, combine the flour, baking powder, and salt. Add the milk, melted butter, and egg. Stir until the dough comes together.

TO ASSEMBLE

Keeping the broth to a simmer, drop in the dumpling dough, 1 tablespoon (or use a 2-inch cookie scoop) at a time. Cover the pot and simmer the dumplings over low heat for 10 to 15 minutes, until they are light and fluffy on the outside and tender on the inside. Add the chicken pieces to the pot and give a gentle stir. Continue cooking until the chicken is hot, about 10 minutes. Stir occasionally to prevent the dumplings from scorching. Gently stir in the tarragon.

SMOTHERED FRIED CHICKEN
WITH ANDOUILLE SAUSAGE

The smoky, spicy flavors of andouille sausage give this smothered chicken its distinctive flavor and richness. Serve this over Carolina Gold Rice and you will bring a combination of Cajun and the Low Country to your table.

NOTE: If you do not have self-rising flour, add 1 teaspoon baking powder and ¼ teaspoon salt to each cup of all-purpose flour.

SERVES 4

FOR THE CHICKEN

1 whole chicken (3½ to 3¾ pounds)
4 cups cold water
2½ teaspoons salt
4 cups self-rising flour (see Note)
1 teaspoon freshly ground black pepper
Vegetable oil for frying

FOR THE GRAVY

¼ cup vegetable oil
½ cup self-rising flour
2 cups water, more if needed
1 fresh andouille sausage link (about ⅓ pound), removed from casing

TO MAKE THE FRIED CHICKEN

Cut the chicken into 8 pieces, then cut the breast pieces in half crosswise to make 10 pieces, which makes for a quicker frying time. Prepare the brine. In a large bowl, combine the cold water, 2 teaspoons of the salt, and ice. Place the chicken pieces in the brine, cover, and refrigerate for 1 hour or overnight.

In a medium bowl, combine the 4 cups of flour, the remaining ½ teaspoon of salt, and the pepper. Fill a large skillet one-third full of oil, or until about 2 inches deep. Heat the oil to 325°F (medium). Remove the chicken pieces from the brine, letting excess water drip off each piece. Dredge the wet chicken pieces in the flour mixture 1 piece at a time. Shake off any excess flour and, working quickly, place each piece of chicken in the oil. Fry the chicken pieces in one layer, skin side up, until they start to brown, then gently flip to the opposite side. Keep turning the pieces occasionally until golden brown, about 15 minutes for breast and wings, and about 20 minutes for thighs. The internal temperature of the chicken should be a minimum of 165°F. You may need to adjust the oil temperature from medium to medium-low as the temperature will increase as you remove pieces of cooked chicken from the oil. Place them on paper towels as you remove them from the oil. Pat off the oil. Keep warm.

TO MAKE THE GRAVY

Place the pan back on medium heat and add the ¼ cup vegetable oil to the skillet. Heat the oil over medium-low heat. Add the ½ cup flour and stir to blend until the roux is golden brown, 5 to 10 minutes. Whisk in the water and continue whisking until the mixture is smooth and has thickened. Continue cooking for 5 minutes. If the gravy becomes too thick, whisk in a little water. Add the sausage and simmer for 2 minutes.

Place the fried chicken pieces in the skillet with the gravy. Spoon the gravy over the top of the chicken to coat it. Simmer for 5 minutes.

CHICKEN CROQUETTES
WITH BUTTER AND HERB CREAM SAUCE

With their crispy, golden crust and moist, creamy center, chicken croquettes are one of my favorite dishes—especially the way Mama made them. Serve them over Carolina Gold Rice and spoon the herb butter sauce over the top for an elegant main course for special occasions. For a casual weeknight meal, place them atop Caesar salad. Use a rotisserie chicken for a time-saving preparation.

SERVES 6

FOR THE CROQUETTES

- 3 tablespoons unsalted butter
- 3 tablespoons all-purpose flour
- 1 teaspoon salt
- 1 cup milk
- 3 cups chopped cooked chicken
- ½ cup mushrooms, finely chopped
- 1 tablespoon onion, minced
- 1 tablespoon chopped fresh Italian parsley
- 3 egg yolks
- 2 tablespoons water
- 2 cups bread crumbs
- Vegetable oil for frying

FOR THE BUTTER AND HERB CREAM SAUCE

- ¼ cup finely chopped shallots
- ½ cup heavy cream
- 1 tablespoon fresh lemon juice
- 1 cup dry white wine
- 1 tablespoon finely chopped fresh rosemary
- 1 cup (2 sticks) unsalted butter, chilled

TO MAKE THE CROQUETTES

In a large skillet over medium heat, melt the butter. Stir in the flour and salt. Add the milk and stir until the mixture is smooth and has thickened, 1 to 2 minutes. Remove from the heat and let cool. Add the chicken, mushrooms, onion, and parsley. Shape the mixture into croquettes and refrigerate them for at least 2 hours.

recipe continues →

When you are ready to fry the croquettes, beat together the egg yolks and water. Quickly dip each croquette in the beaten egg mixture and then coat with the bread crumbs. Fry the croquettes in the vegetable oil over medium heat on both sides until they are golden brown, 4 to 6 minutes.

TO MAKE THE BUTTER AND HERB CREAM SAUCE

Place the shallots, cream, lemon juice, and wine in a medium saucepan over medium heat. Bring to a simmer, stirring occasionally until the liquid is reduced by half, 10 to 15 minutes. Stir in the rosemary.

Remove from the heat. Add the butter, 4 tablespoons at a time, whisking after each addition until the butter is melted before adding more. Keep warm over hot but not boiling water until ready to serve.

FRIED GREEN TOMATO PARMESAN

This recipe is a Southern take on the classic Italian dish. The tartness of the fried green tomatoes steps in naturally for the traditional chicken, creating a welcoming option for vegetarians at your table.

SERVES 6

- 6 medium green tomatoes
- 1 cup cornmeal
- ½ cup self-rising flour
- 1½ cups grated Parmesan cheese
- 1 teaspoon salt
- 2 cups milk
- 2 eggs, beaten
- Vegetable oil for frying
- 1 (28-ounce) can crushed tomatoes
- ¼ cup chopped fresh basil
- 2 cups (½ pound) grated mozzarella cheese

Wash the tomatoes. Remove the stem ends and cut each tomato into four slices. In a medium bowl, combine the cornmeal, flour, ½ cup of the Parmesan cheese, and salt. In a separate small bowl, beat together the milk and eggs. Dip the tomato slices in the milk mixture, then dredge in the flour mixture. Repeat until all the tomatoes are coated. Place the coated tomato slices on a sheet pan in one layer.

Fill a large skillet with oil to a depth of ½ inch and heat over medium heat. In batches, fry the tomato slices on each side until golden brown, 2 minutes per side. Drain them on paper towels. Layer half of the fried tomato slices in the bottom of a 2-quart casserole or baking dish. Spoon half of the crushed tomatoes over the top and cover them with half of the basil, half of the remaining Parmesan cheese, and half of the mozzarella cheese. Repeat layers, ending with the cheese.

Preheat the oven to 375°F. Bake uncovered for 15 to 20 minutes. Your Fried Green Tomato Parmesan is ready when everything is heated through and the cheese is completely melted.

CAROLINA BURGER

My grandfather offered hamburgers, cheeseburgers, and his signature Bill's Big Burger—a large patty spread with Thousand Island dressing and topped with lettuce, tomato, and onions and served on an oversized bun. But, back in the day, if you wanted to get a delicious all-the-way burger experience, you would order a chili cheeseburger, which I now refer to as the Carolina Burger.

SERVES 4

FOR THE BURGER

- 1 pound ground beef (80/20)
- ½ teaspoon salt
- ½ teaspoon granulated garlic
- 4 slices cheddar cheese
- 4 tablespoons mayonnaise
- 4 hamburger buns, toasted and buttered
- Coleslaw (recipe follows)
- 1 small onion, chopped
- Chili (recipe follows)

FOR THE CHILI

- ½ pound ground beef (80/20)
- 2 tablespoons chopped onion
- ½ cup ketchup
- ½ teaspoon chili powder

FOR THE COLESLAW

- 2 cups finely grated cabbage (about ½ small cabbage)
- ¼ cup mayonnaise
- 2 teaspoons apple cider vinegar
- 2 teaspoons sugar

TO MAKE THE BURGER

Combine the ground beef, salt, and garlic in a medium bowl. Divide the seasoned beef into four equal balls. Press each ball into a patty. In a large skillet, fry the patties on medium-high on each side for 4 to 5 minutes for well done. Place a slice of cheese on top of each burger.

TO MAKE THE CHILI

Crumble the ground beef and brown with the onion in a medium saucepan over medium heat, 7 to 10 minutes. Add the ketchup and chili powder and stir to combine. Let the chili simmer over low heat for 1 minute. Skim off excess fat.

TO MAKE THE COLESLAW

Combine the cabbage, mayonnaise, vinegar, and sugar in a medium bowl. Mix together until the sugar dissolves. Cover and refrigerate for at least 30 minutes.

TO ASSEMBLE

Spread mayonnaise on the toasted hamburger buns. Layer the flat side with coleslaw, onion, chili, and a cheeseburger. Top with the other half of the bun.

PINTO BEAN BOWL

WITH FATBACK CORN BREAD CRUMBLE AND ONION JAM

Pinto beans were a staple on the back burners of stovetops in my youth. A pot of beans could feed a crowd and supply nourishment when parents were at work. My grandfather served a bowl of pintos topped with chopped raw onions, two hush puppies, and a thick slice of crispy fried fatback at his restaurant, Bill's Bar-B-Q. It was on the top sellers list. Replacing the hush puppies with fatback corn bread crumble, and the raw onions with onion jam takes the flavors to another level of taste.

SERVES 8

FOR THE PINTO BEANS

- 1 (16-ounce) package dried pinto beans
- 1 smoked ham hock
- 2 teaspoons granulated garlic
- 2 teaspoons granulated onion
- 1 tablespoon fresh minced savory leaves or 1½ teaspoons dried savory leaves
- 2 teaspoons salt

FOR THE FATBACK CORN BREAD CRUMBLE

- 3¼-inch slices fatback
- 1 cup cornmeal
- ½ cup self-rising flour
- 1 teaspoon sugar
- 1 cup buttermilk
- 1 egg
- 2 tablespoons unsalted butter, melted

TO MAKE THE PINTO BEANS

Pick over the beans for small rocks or debris. Rinse well and cover with cold water and soak for 6 hours or overnight. Transfer the beans to a stockpot or Dutch oven. Add the ham hock and enough water to cover the beans by 2 inches. Bring to a boil. Reduce to a simmer and cook the beans, stirring occasionally, for 1½ hours. Add the garlic, onion, savory, and salt and continue cooking until tender and creamy, about 30 minutes.

TO MAKE THE FATBACK CORN BREAD CRUMBLE

Preheat the oven to 350°F.

Fry the fatback on each side in a small skillet over medium heat until crispy, 30 to 40 seconds on each side. Drain on paper towels. When cool enough to handle, chop the fat portion into small pieces. Pour the fat rendered from the fatback into an 8-inch square baking pan. Set aside. Combine the cornmeal, flour, and sugar in a medium bowl. Add the buttermilk and egg and stir until combined. Pour into the greased baking pan, and bake for 25 to 30 minutes, or until golden brown.

When the corn bread is cool enough to handle, grate it against the large hole of a box grater. Place the crumbs in a small bowl. Add the butter and toss to coat. Spread the buttered crumbs onto a baking sheet and toast in the oven for 5 to 10 minutes until crisped.

TO ASSEMBLE

Spoon warm pinto beans into your serving dish or bowls. Top with the Fatback Corn Bread Crumble and add a layer of Onion Jam. Serve immediately.

ONION JAM

MAKES ABOUT 2 CUPS

- 4 tablespoons unsalted butter
- 2 medium onions, halved and thinly sliced
- ¼ cup apple cider vinegar
- 3 tablespoons light brown sugar
- 2 bay leaves
- ½ teaspoon salt
- ½ teaspoon white pepper

In a medium skillet over medium heat, melt the butter. Add the onions and stir occasionally, until the onions are translucent, about 5 minutes. Add the vinegar and brown sugar. Stir until the sugar dissolves. Add the remaining ingredients and simmer for 25 to 30 minutes, until the liquid evaporates. Remove the bay leaves.

EGGPLANT AND TOMATO CASSEROLE

This dish adds eggplant, one of my favorite vegetables, to a traditional stewed tomato casserole. It works well as a hearty vegetarian main course or as a flavorful side dish.

SERVES 8

- 2 (14.5-ounce) cans diced tomatoes
- ¼ cup light brown sugar, packed
- 1 teaspoon freshly ground black pepper
- ¼ teaspoon salt
- 4 tablespoons unsalted butter, melted
- 1 large eggplant (about 1 pound), cut into cubes
- 1 cup bread cubes

Preheat the oven to 350°F.

Place the tomatoes, brown sugar, pepper, salt, and butter in a large bowl and stir to combine. Fold in the eggplant and bread cubes. Pour the mixture into a 3-quart baking dish. Bake for 30 to 40 minutes, or until the mixture is bubbly and the bread cubes are golden brown.

COME SUNDAY

SUNDAY WAS THE DAY for church service, eating and gathering, visiting and having visitors, resting and relaxing. We knew it had arrived when the radio, tuned in to the gospel music channel, awakened us to the rhythmic sound waves of the gospel artist Reverend James Cleveland singing "A Good Day." The music mixed with the fragrance of buttery grits, cured bacon, peppery sausage, smoky fatback—left over from cooking greens the night before—flaky biscuits, and the sweet smell of molasses.

I would open my eyes and listen to the music. I took my time, enjoying the ambiance of Sunday morning, knowing that breakfast wasn't going anywhere. But when I heard the upbeat song "Oh Happy Day," by The Edwin Hawkins Singers, I knew it was time to get moving and get dressed to attend Hamlet Chapel CME Church and then eat a hearty meal.

After church, we sat down to enjoy Sunday supper, a day when food was available all day. The stovetop held pots of food, while the oven door was opened and rested on its hinges, its racks extended to use as a buffet table.

Mama spent Saturday evening preparing most of our Sunday dinner—a slow pot roast with root vegetables, roast beef with Yorkshire pudding, fried chicken, two or three side dishes, and dessert. On those days when Mama would talk about creating her menu and not knowing what she should prepare, I would quickly request one of my favorite dishes. I would repeatedly ask with a "Please, please, Mama—Mama please!" until she agreed. I am getting hungry writing about it.

As Mr. Bynum Weaver, the proprietor of our neighborhood store, used to say, "It tastes so good that it will make you fight your grandmother." That was his pitch for the cookies he sold. We knew nothing existed to make us fight our grandmother, but the cookies he sold tasted good.

There were many dishes on my request list. Chicken pudding was one of them, and Mama had a way of creating the perfect balance of bread and sauce. Then there was her field peas and corn—the best—and braised beef short ribs.

I still keep the "Come Sunday" tradition by tuning to the local gospel station, stepping into my kitchen, and cooking up food memories.

BRAISED BEEF SHORT RIBS

These ribs are one of my favorite dishes. The slow, long simmer creates a rich gravy and tender bites of beef that fall away from the bone. Eating them brings back memories of the first time Mama served me a plate of mouthwatering braised beef short ribs. Serve this dish with Mashed Potatoes and Turnips with Thyme Butter (page 149) for a heartwarming meal.

SERVES 6

4 pounds beef short ribs
1 teaspoon salt
½ teaspoon freshly ground black pepper
2 cups self-rising flour
¼ cup vegetable oil
2 garlic cloves, crushed
3 star anise
8 cups beef broth
10 ounces pearl onions, blanched in boiling water for 1 minute, and peeled

Season the ribs with salt and pepper, then dredge them in the flour. In a large pot, heat the oil over medium heat. Add the ribs in a single layer and brown them on all sides. Once the ribs are browned, remove them from the pot and set aside on a platter. Pour off all but 2 tablespoons of the fat from the pot. Reduce the heat to medium-low. Add the garlic and star anise to the pot and cook for 1 minute. Return the ribs to the pot, add the beef broth, and bring to a boil over medium-high heat. Reduce the heat to a simmer and cook for 1½ to 2 hours. Add the pearl onions 15 minutes before the ribs are fall-off-the-bone tender.

COLLARDS AND ITALIAN SAUSAGE LASAGNA

My Uncle Jim raised pigs and chickens on his farm, often feeding them leftovers from the Rathskeller, a restaurant where he worked as a cook for many years. Sometimes, he'd come get me and my siblings in his pickup truck, and we'd ride in the bed to help him feed the hogs. One of their favorite treats was baked potatoes, foil and all. I remember asking if we should remove the foil, and Uncle Jim said, "No, they like to lick the foil!" It was so much fun hanging out at Uncle Jim's farm, and I remember those visits as his way of spending quality time with us.

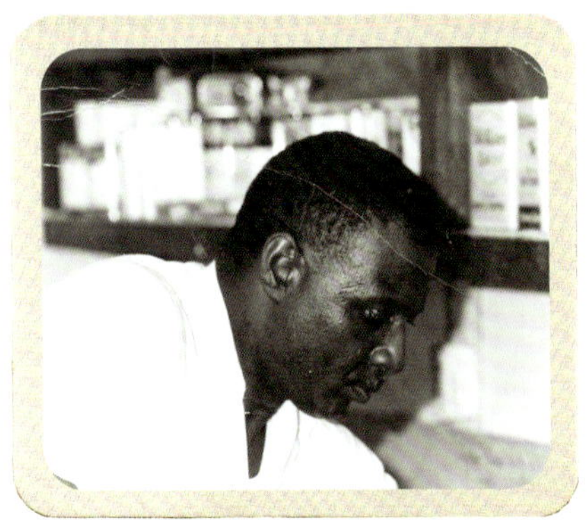

At Christmas, Uncle Jim would come to the window of our home, claiming to be Santa Claus. Every child knew you didn't want to be awake when Santa arrived, because he would put pepper in your eyes. We'd run screaming, and he'd have a jolly laugh while giving us big hugs.

This lasagna is cheesy, just like the one Uncle Jim made at the Rathskeller. He used ground beef, but I replaced it with collard greens and spicy Italian sausage to give the dish a little kick. Different, but equally tasty.

SERVES 8

- 9 (8 ounces) wide lasagna noodles
- 1 medium onion, finely chopped
- 2 garlic cloves, minced
- 2 tablespoons olive oil
- 2 spicy Italian sausage links, removed from casing
- 1 (14.5-ounce) can diced tomatoes, drained
- 1 (24-ounce) jar pasta sauce
- 2 teaspoons dried basil
- 1 teaspoon dried oregano
- ½ cup grated Parmesan cheese
- 1 cup ricotta cheese
- 2 egg yolks
- 2 cups cooked collard greens
- 8 ounces mozzarella cheese, sliced
- 8 ounces provolone cheese, sliced

recipe continues →

Preheat the oven to 350°F.

Cook the lasagna noodles in boiling salted water until al dente, 10 to 12 minutes, stirring frequently to prevent sticking. Drain and add cold water to cool. Drain and place the noodles on a baking sheet lined with parchment paper and cover with a kitchen towel.

Sauté the onion and garlic in the olive oil over medium-low heat in a large skillet until the onion is soft but not browned, about 5 minutes. Stir in the sausage and cook until browned, 2 to 3 minutes. Drain the oil from the sausage. Add the tomatoes, pasta sauce, basil, and oregano to the sausage mixture. Bring to a simmer and cook for 10 minutes, stirring occasionally.

In a small bowl, combine the Parmesan cheese, ricotta cheese, and egg yolks. Line the bottom of a 13-by-9-by-2 baking pan with 3 lasagna noodles. Spread half of the ricotta mixture first, then half of the meat sauce, half of the collards, a layer of mozzarella, and a layer of provolone and top with 3 lasagna noodles. Repeat laying the ricotta mixture, meat sauce, collards, mozzarella, and provolone. Finish by topping with 3 noodles and ending with a layer of provolone cheese on top.

Bake uncovered for 25 to 30 minutes. Your lasagna is ready when everything is heated through and the cheese is completely melted. Let it rest for 15 minutes before serving.

COUNTRY-STYLE PORK SPARE RIBS

I always enjoyed indulging in the barbecue pork ribs at Mama Dip's Kitchen. Sometimes, now, I can't resist sneaking a few before the sauce is added to my own country-style version of Mama's dish. It's absolutely delicious!

SERVES 6

- 4 to 5 pounds pork spare ribs
- 2 tablespoons granulated garlic
- 1 tablespoon onion powder
- 2 teaspoons salt
- 2 teaspoons black pepper
- 2 tablespoons olive oil
- 3 medium onions, sliced
- 2 tablespoons all-purpose flour
- 2 jalapeño peppers, seeded and diced

Preheat the oven to 350°F. Remove excess fat from the ribs and cut between them to separate. Place the ribs in a large pot and cover with water. Add the granulated garlic, onion powder, salt, and pepper and bring to a boil. Reduce the heat to a simmer and cook for 1½ hours, or until the ribs are tender. Drain the liquid from the ribs, reserving 1 cup. Strain the cup of liquid. Place the ribs in a large oven-safe casserole dish. Set aside.

Heat the olive oil over low heat in a medium saucepan. Add the onions and sauté until translucent, about 5 minutes. Whisk the flour into the onion mixture, stirring constantly, until the flour is golden brown, 5 to 10 minutes. Gradually add the reserved broth, stirring constantly. Add the jalapeño peppers. Pour the gravy over the pork ribs. Bake for 15 minutes, or until the ribs are hot.

PAN-FRIED LAMB CHOPS

The combination of Italian Parmesan cheese and Southern biscuit crumb coating makes these lamb chops a tasty combination of Old World meets New World. This simple and easy-to-prepare recipe pairs well with Eggplant and Tomato Casserole (page 126).

SERVES 4

8 lamb rib chops
¼ teaspoon salt
3 tablespoons unsalted butter, softened
2 tablespoons biscuit crumbs
1 cup all-purpose flour
¼ cup grated Parmesan cheese
¼ cup milk
1 egg, beaten
Vegetable oil

Season the lamb chops with the salt. Brush the lamb chops with the butter on all sides. Combine the biscuit crumbs, flour, and Parmesan cheese in a shallow bowl. In another shallow bowl, mix together the milk and egg. Dip the lamb chops into the egg mixture, then coat them with the biscuit crumb mixture. Pour ½ to 1 inch of oil into a large skillet. The oil should reach about half the depth of the lamb chops. Heat the oil to 350°F and fry the lamb chops in batches for 3 to 4 minutes on each side, or until cooked to your desired level of doneness.

PECAN AND HERB-CRUSTED SALMON

In this dish, the toasted pecans bring a sweet nuttiness that goes well with the delicate flavor of the salmon, while the herbs add a touch of freshness. To present this showstopper, arrange it on a large platter or wooden board and garnish it with fresh herb sprigs and lemon slices for an ideal centerpiece on your buffet table. You will need an oversize spatula to transfer the salmon onto the platter in one piece.

SERVES 8 TO 10

- 3 teaspoons olive oil, plus more for the baking sheet
- 1 (3-pound) boneless salmon fillet
- 1 garlic clove, finely chopped
- 1 teaspoon salt
- ½ teaspoon freshly ground black pepper
- Juice of 1 lemon
- 2 cups pecans, chopped
- 1 tablespoon fresh thyme leaves
- 2 tablespoons finely chopped fresh dill

Preheat the oven to 425°F.

Brush a baking pan lightly with olive oil. Lay the salmon on the baking pan with the skin side down. Rub the top side of the salmon with 1 teaspoon of the olive oil and the garlic. Sprinkle the salt, pepper, and lemon juice on top. Bake for 15 minutes.

In a small bowl, combine the pecans, thyme, and the remaining 2 teaspoons of the olive oil. Remove the salmon from the oven and coat the top evenly with the pecan mixture. Return the salmon to the oven and continue cooking for 5 minutes longer, or until the pecans are toasted. Remove from the oven and sprinkle the dill evenly over the top. Use two large spatulas to transfer the salmon without the skin from the baking pan to a platter in one piece.

SHRIMP POTATO SALAD

Southern-style potato salad is simply delicious with the addition of shrimp. This main course is great to serve on a buffet table.

SERVES 6 TO 8

1½ pounds medium shrimp, peeled and deveined

½ teaspoon salt, plus more for the pot

1 pound Yukon Gold potatoes

¼ cup celery, diced

¼ cup sweet pickle relish

2 tablespoons chopped fresh Italian parsley

2 hard-boiled eggs, grated

¾ cup mayonnaise

1 teaspoon yellow mustard

Boil the shrimp in salted water just until the shrimp turns pink. Drain the water.

Place the potatoes in a large pot and add enough water to cover them by 1 inch. Bring the water to a boil and cook the potatoes until they are tender, 15 to 20 minutes. Peel and dice the potatoes.

In a large bowl, combine the shrimp, potatoes, celery, relish, parsley, eggs, mayonnaise, mustard, and ½ teaspoon salt. Chill the salad in the refrigerator for at least 2 hours.

SHRIMP CROQUETTES

WITH REMOULADE COLESLAW ON A BUN

Working at Mama Dip's Kitchen, I got to know many of our customers, and a few became friends outside of work—like Jim Rumfelt, owner of The Clean Machine bicycle shop in Carrboro. My sister Lane and I even bartered with him for our 10-speed bikes. Eventually, Jim invited me to join a group of cyclists on his annual ride through the Outer Banks. He didn't believe I'd go—until I showed up, ready to ride.

That trip tested my endurance with headwinds and long stretches of road, but the reward was unforgettable food. In Morehead City, Jim led us to El's Drive-In, where I had my first shrimp burger—crispy fried shrimp, coleslaw, tartar sauce, and ketchup on a steamed hamburger bun. This croquette sandwich is my take on that classic: sautéed shrimp bound with a white sauce, coated in cracker crumbs, fried to a crispy crust, and served with a creamy remoulade coleslaw. This dish has no other choice but to tickle your taste buds.

SERVES 4

FOR THE CROQUETTES

4 tablespoons unsalted butter

½ cup red onion, finely chopped

1 garlic clove, minced

1 teaspoon salt

1 pound shrimp, peeled and deveined

¼ cup flour

1 cup milk

Vegetable oil for frying

1 cup cracker crumbs

1 cup cornmeal

4 hamburger buns, buttered and toasted

Remoulade Coleslaw (recipe follows)

FOR THE REMOULADE COLESLAW

½ of a small, lightweight cabbage, cored and finely shredded (about 2 cups)

¼ cup mayonnaise

½ teaspoon mustard

2 tablespoons sweet pickle relish

1 tablespoon capers

recipe continues →

TO MAKE THE CROQUETTES

Melt the butter in a large skillet over medium-low heat. Add the onion, garlic, and salt. Cook, stirring frequently, for 8 to 10 minutes, until tender but not brown. Add the shrimp and sauté until it turns pink. Add the flour and stir to coat the shrimp. Add the milk and stir until thickened. Chill in the refrigerator for 2 hours or overnight.

Coat the bottom of a large skillet with 1 inch of vegetable oil. Heat the vegetable oil to 325°F. In a shallow bowl, combine the cracker crumbs and cornmeal. Shape the shrimp mixture into 4 patties and coat with the cracker crumb mixture. Fry in the oil for 2 to 3 minutes on each side, or until golden brown.

TO MAKE THE REMOULADE COLESLAW

Place the prepared cabbage in a medium bowl. Add the mayonnaise, mustard, relish, and capers. Stir until combined.

TO ASSEMBLE

Place a shrimp croquette on the bottom half of the bun. Top with a heaping spoon of coleslaw and the top bun.

HOLIDAYS AT HOME

FRIED WALNUTS

Mama enjoyed old-fashioned Christmas traditions. Her version of holiday decorating included stringing popcorn on thread to use as a garland, and positioning the paper ornaments we made at school at the front of the tree. She also filled brown paper bags with unshelled mixed nuts, including walnuts, plus apples, oranges, and hard candy. We would eat the sweet, fragrant orange wedges together with the walnuts in one mouthful. In this recipe, the aromatic flavor of zested orange peel stands out between the crunch of the fried walnuts. It's hard to stop eating them. They bring back delightful memories of those simple, delicious goodies stuffed in a brown paper bag.

MAKES ABOUT 2 CUPS

- 4 tablespoons sugar
- ½ teaspoon white pepper
- 2 cups raw walnut halves
- 2 cups vegetable oil
- 2 tablespoons finely grated orange zest
- ⅛ teaspoon coarse sea salt

Combine the sugar and pepper in a medium bowl. Bring 4 cups of water to a boil in a medium saucepan over high heat. Add the walnuts and cook for 1 minute. Use a slotted spoon to lift the walnuts out of the water and toss them into the sugar mixture, making sure all the walnuts are completely coated.

Heat the oil to 325°F in a medium saucepan. Add half of the sugar-coated walnuts and cook them for 1 to 2 minutes, until golden brown. Stir to keep the walnuts from sticking together. Using a slotted spoon, remove the walnuts from the oil, drain them on a paper towel for a second, then remove them to a medium bowl before they stick to the paper towel. Repeat until all are cooked.

Place the fried walnuts in the bowl. Add the orange zest and salt and toss to mix in with the fried walnuts.

MAMA'S GRILLED CORN ON THE COB

One Fourth of July, Mama told me she was making a corn recipe and sent me on a shopping errand to purchase Parmesan cheese, parsley, and mayonnaise. She had already purchased corn from the farmers' market. This recipe is her version of Mexican street corn. It was her first time making it and my first time eating it, and it became a staple for our Fourth of July cookouts for years to come.

SERVES 6 TO 8

- 8 ears of corn
- 1 cup mayonnaise
- 1 cup grated Parmesan cheese
- ½ cup finely chopped fresh Italian parsley

Pull the husk back from each ear of corn and remove the silk, leaving the corn husk attached. Pull the husk back over the corn and soak it in cold water for 30 minutes. Remove the corn from the water and shake off excess.

Meanwhile, preheat the outdoor grill to medium heat. Place the corn on the grill and cook, turning often, until lightly charred and tender. Remove the corn from the grill, let cool enough to handle, and remove the husks.

Spread each ear of corn with mayonnaise, sprinkle Parmesan cheese over the mayonnaise, and place on a large shallow pan in one layer. Place the pan on the grill for 10 to 12 minutes, or until the cheese is melted. Remove from the heat and sprinkle each ear with parsley.

SWEET POTATO HOT CROSS BUNS

Baked sweet potatoes add natural sweetness and moisture to these delicious Easter buns, making them a perfect twist on a traditional favorite.

MAKES 12 BUNS

FOR THE BUNS

- 1 medium sweet potato
- 1½ cups milk
- 4 tablespoons unsalted butter
- 1 teaspoon salt
- ½ cup sugar
- 1 teaspoon vanilla extract
- 2 (¼-ounce) packages active dry yeast
- ¼ cup warm water (105° to 115°F)
- 4 cups all-purpose flour
- 1 teaspoon ground cinnamon
- 3 eggs, beaten
- ¾ cup currants
- Oil for the bowl

FOR THE CROSSES

- 1 cup confectioners' sugar
- 5 teaspoons milk
- 2 teaspoons finely grated orange zest

TO MAKE THE BUNS

Preheat oven to 400°F. Bake the sweet potato until it is done but still firm, 35 to 45 minutes. Cool, peel, and dice it. Set it aside.

Heat the milk, butter, salt, and sugar in a medium saucepan over medium heat until the sugar dissolves. Remove the mixture from the heat and let it cool until it is lukewarm. Stir in the vanilla. Dissolve the yeast in the warm water. Add the yeast mixture to the milk mixture. Whisk together the flour and cinnamon in a large bowl. Make a well in the center of the flour mixture and pour in the milk mixture and eggs. Stir until a dough forms. Place the dough on a floured surface. Pat it into a disk and place the diced sweet potato and currants on top. Knead them into the dough until the dough is smooth. Transfer the dough to a large oiled bowl and lightly coat the top with oil. Cover the bowl with plastic wrap and set it in a warm place for about an hour or until the dough doubles in size.

Shape the dough into 12 equally sized balls. Place them on a greased baking pan. Cover them with plastic and let them rise in a warm place for about 45 minutes, until doubled in size. Preheat the oven to 375°F. Bake the buns for 15 to 20 minutes, or until they are golden brown. Let them cool to room temperature.

TO MAKE THE CROSSES

Mix together the confectioners' sugar and milk in a small bowl until the mixture is smooth. Stir in the orange zest. Spoon the mixture into a piping bag and pipe a cross design on the top of each bun.

MASHED POTATOES AND TURNIPS

WITH THYME BUTTER

This side dish is easy to prepare and goes well with lamb and roasted pork. I prefer to use small turnip roots, as they are milder than the larger ones and blend well with the potatoes. The larger turnips are spicier, but when combined with potatoes, they mellow out and give the dish a sweet and earthy flavor.

SERVES 6

FOR THE THYME BUTTER

½ cup (1 stick) salted butter, at room temperature

1 tablespoon chopped fresh thyme leaves

½ teaspoon granulated garlic

FOR THE POTATOES

1½ pounds Yukon Gold potatoes

1½ pounds turnip roots

4 tablespoons unsalted butter, softened

2 tablespoons warm milk

1 teaspoon salt

TO MAKE THE THYME BUTTER

In a small bowl, whip the butter until creamy. Add the thyme and granulated garlic and stir to combine. Place the butter mixture in the center of a large piece of plastic wrap or parchment paper and form into a log. Twist the ends until tight. Chill in the refrigerator for at least 2 hours.

TO MAKE THE POTATOES

Peel and cut the potatoes and turnips into similarly sized chunks. Bring water to a boil in a medium saucepan. Reduce the heat to a simmer and add the potatoes and turnips together and cook until tender, 10 to 15 minutes. Drain the liquid well. Add the butter, milk, and salt. Mash the potatoes and turnips together until they are smooth. Serve the thyme butter on the side.

OKRA AND BLACK-EYED PEAS PILAF

This dish combines two South Carolina Lowcountry rice dishes: Limpin' Susan, which consists of rice and okra, and Hoppin' John, which combines black-eyed peas and rice. I heard a folktale that Limpin' Susan is the wife of Hoppin' John, so I decided to bring them together in this marriage of flavors.

SERVES 8 TO 10

- 1 smoked ham hock
- 2 cup dried black-eyed peas, washed and sorted
- ½ teaspoon crushed red pepper
- 1 teaspoon granulated garlic
- 1 teaspoon salt
- 2 cups cooked rice
- 1 (12-ounce) package frozen cut okra

Add the ham hock, black-eyed peas, crushed red pepper, granulated garlic, and salt to a medium saucepan. Add enough water to cover the peas by 2 inches. Bring the water to a boil. Reduce the heat and simmer for 1 to 1½ hours, or until the peas are tender. Stir the rice and okra into the peas and cook over low heat, stirring often, until the rice and okra are hot, about 10 minutes.

A SOUTHERN NEW YEAR

MAMA DECIDED TO START the tradition of offering customers a taste of a Southern New Year's Day meal. To season her black-eyed peas, she needed a smoked hog jaw. She asked me to purchase it at a butcher shop in downtown Durham. I had never bought a hog jaw before, but I was up for the task. I drove to Durham, went inside the store, walked to the meat counter in back, pointed to what I thought was a good size jaw, and ordered it. The attendant placed it in a large brown paper bag, and I left the store to drive back to Chapel Hill.

The most memorable part of the experience was that as I was walking along the sidewalk to my car, it felt like the bag itself was invisible in my hand, as if everyone nearby could see right through it—straight to the smoked, cured half of a hog's head, molar still attached. It just felt different walking along the street with a hog's jaw in a brown paper bag.

But I can tell you this—those were the tastiest, richest, smokiest-flavored black-eyed peas I had ever had, and eating them definitely gave one good luck for the year.

From that first New Year's Day on, it became the busiest day of the year for the restaurant. Southerners and non-Southerners alike eagerly took part in the traditional New Year's Day meal at Mama Dip's Kitchen—roasted pork for good health, black-eyed peas for good luck, collard greens for lots of money, and candied yams that Mama added to the mix to bring sweetness to the meal.

SWISS CHARD AND CHICKPEA BREAD AND BUTTER PUDDING

This savory bread pudding goes well with roasted turkey and roasted leg of lamb. Vegetarians at the table will appreciate it, too, because it's high in protein. Plus, it's a breeze to make.

SERVES 8 TO 10

- 2 tablespoons olive oil
- 1 medium yellow onion, chopped
- 1 garlic clove, minced
- 2 large bunches Swiss chard, stems removed and chopped
- 3 cups milk
- 6 eggs, beaten
- 1 teaspoon salt, or to taste
- ½ teaspoon white pepper
- 2 cups biscuits or baguette, cut into cubes
- 4 tablespoons unsalted butter, melted
- 1 (15-ounce) can chickpeas, drained and well rinsed

Preheat the oven to 350°F.

In a medium skillet, heat the olive oil over medium heat. Add the onion and cook until the onion is translucent, about 5 minutes. Add the garlic and cook with the onion for 1 minute. Add the chard and cook until wilted, 3 to 5 minutes. Let cool.

In a medium bowl, whisk together the milk, eggs, salt, and pepper. Arrange the bread cubes in the bottom of a 2-quart casserole dish. Pour the melted butter over the bread cubes and toss together until the bread cubes are evenly coated with the butter. Add the chard mixture, along with the chickpeas, to the milk mixture. Pour over the buttered bread cubes and stir to distribute the chard evenly with the bread cubes.

Bake for 50 to 60 minutes, or until the tip of a knife inserted comes out clean and the bread is golden brown and the top is puffed.

CORN BREAD AND PICKLE-CRUSTED BONE-IN SPIRAL CUT HAM

This is my version of old-fashioned stuffed ham. Rather than stuffing the meat, I use the additional flavors as a coating. The ham is first covered with mustard (as an adhesive), baked, and then topped with a combination of corn bread crumbs and bread-and-butter pickles, giving this ham a sweet-and-sour crispy topping. Your holiday meal preparation never had it so easy and tasty.

SERVES 12

½ cup water

1 fully cooked spiral ham (6 to 7 pounds)

2 tablespoons prepared mustard

1 cup bread-and-butter pickles, finely chopped

2 cups corn bread crumbs

Preheat the oven to 325°F.

Pour the water into a roasting pan and place the ham fat side up. Coat the ham with the mustard. Combine the pickles and corn bread crumbs in a medium bowl. Cover the ham with the mixture, pressing down well to make the crumbs adhere to the mustard.

Cover the dish with foil. Bake the ham for 10 to 12 minutes per pound, until the internal temperature reaches 140°F. Remove the foil for the last 20 minutes and continue cooking the ham until the corn bread crumbs are toasted.

PRIME RIB ROAST

WITH YORKSHIRE PUDDING

At my request, Mama would make roast beef with Yorkshire pudding. My taste buds were in heaven the first time I bit into puffy, golden Yorkshire pudding—its moist interior and crispy outer crust formed by cooking in the roast's drippings in a muffin pan.

NOTE: When purchasing a rib roast, allow approximately 1 pound per person.

SERVES 6

FOR THE ROAST

1 (8-pound) standing rib roast, bone cut away from the roast

3 garlic cloves, peeled and sliced

3 tablespoons salt

2 tablespoons freshly ground mixed peppercorns

FOR THE YORKSHIRE PUDDING

4 eggs, beaten

3 cups whole milk

2 cups all-purpose flour

1½ teaspoons coarse salt

¾ cup pan drippings, reserved from prime rib roast

TO MAKE THE ROAST

Allow the roast to stand at room temperature for 1 to 2 hours before seasoning.

Preheat the oven to 450°F. Cut slits all over the roast and insert a sliver of garlic into each slit. Sprinkle the roast all over with the salt and pepper. Place the roast fat side up in a roasting pan, put it in the oven, and roast it for 15 minutes. Reduce the heat to 325°F and continue cooking the roast until it reaches your desired temperature (125° to 130°F for medium done), about 1½ to 2 hours. Insert a meat thermometer into the center of the meat to check for doneness. Let the roast rest for 30 minutes before carving. Reserve 6 tablespoons of the pan drippings.

TO MAKE THE YORKSHIRE PUDDING

In a medium bowl, whisk together the eggs and milk. Add the flour and salt and mix until the batter is smooth. Let stand for 30 minutes.

Preheat the oven to 450°F. Pour 1 tablespoon of the roast drippings into each cup of a popover pan, then place in the oven for 5 minutes until the fat is sizzling hot. Remove from the oven and carefully fill each popover cup with an equal amount of batter. Bake until puffed, about 25 minutes. Then reduce the heat to 375°F and bake until golden brown, about 5 minutes. Serve immediately.

BUTTERMILK YEAST ROLLS

Buttermilk gives these yeast rolls a subtle tangy flavor and a light and fluffy texture. These soft rolls, still warm from the oven and brushed with melted butter, are simple goodness that never goes out of style.

MAKES ABOUT 2 DOZEN

- 1 (¼-ounce) package active dry yeast
- ¼ cup warm water, 105° to 110°F
- 2 cups buttermilk, at room temperature
- 1 egg, beaten
- ¼ cup sugar
- ½ teaspoon baking soda
- 1 teaspoon baking powder
- 1 teaspoon salt
- ½ cup (1 stick) plus 3 tablespoons unsalted butter, melted
- 4½ cups all-purpose flour

Preheat the oven to 375°F.

Combine the yeast and warm water in a large mixing bowl. Let stand until the yeast has softened. Add the buttermilk, egg, sugar, baking soda, baking powder, salt, and ½ cup of the melted butter. Mix in 4 cups of the flour. Add enough of the remaining ½ cup flour to create a soft dough. Transfer the dough to a large, lightly greased bowl. Lightly oil the top of the dough and cover it with plastic wrap. Let it stand in a warm place for about 1 hour until it doubles in size.

Turn out the dough onto a floured surface. Knead it until it is smooth. Roll out the dough on a lightly floured surface and use a 2-inch cookie cutter to cut it into rounds. Place the rounds on a greased baking sheet. Bake for 20 to 25 minutes, or until golden brown. Remove the rolls from the oven and brush with the remaining melted butter.

TABLE SETTING

WHEN MY GRANDMOTHER HOSTED her church ladies' auxiliary meetings, I would visit to see her table setting. She adorned her buffet with a polished silver tea set, floral-edged china plates, lace tablecloth, linen napkins, and silver spoons. As a result, I always had a feeling of calm and tranquility. The air there seemed different from the usual hustle and bustle of everyday life living in a large family.

I see each table setting element as a piece of art that someone created, and then I bring them together to build a cohesive tablescape and an enjoyable ambiance to the meal. My mother once told me not to put your fine china and crystal glasses in the cabinet and let them sit there for special occasions only. "Use them as often as you can," she said.

It's about thought and care, making time for family and friends, and it's about creating a calm and welcoming environment. One thing my guests say about me is that I never seem stressed while I am entertaining. I, for one, do not operate well in chaos, so I do a lot of planning beforehand, and then I just roll with the flow and make changes if needed. But my not-so-secret weapon is that I have been working in the restaurant business since I was 12 years old, which helps me perform well in the service department.

Here are some of my favorite tips for creating gracious tablescapes:

- Create your menu first, then choose the setting that will pair with the meal you are serving. For example, I use a large dinner plate with enough room to hold two meats and sides. Some of my china patterns are dainty, but not too delicate to serve fried chicken.
- When styling your dining table, use the same technique you might use when coordinating outfits and do not quite know what to wear. Because we generally pull out different clothing items and accessories with different colors and textures from our closets to try on before making a final decision, do the same for your dining table by having a "dress rehearsal."
- Next, use colors and textures that contrast with your china pattern. Mix bold with bold and dainty with dainty. Play around with different

china, silverware, linens, and glasses on the table to create the look you want to achieve. Then, decide on the centerpiece you want to blend into the design.

- I like to use a mix of patterns and textures. Make sure the hues match: If so, then the combinations are endless.
- At one time, before she began building her inventory of china tableware, my mother had only one piece: a pretty plate. If you, too, have limited china, start with what you have and begin building your collection. Remember, every piece does not have to be from the same pattern.
- I coordinate pieces purchased at thrift shops, yard sales, and estate sales. You will find great bargains shopping at those places.
- Finally, be sure to provide your guests with a delicious meal to accompany your beautiful tablescape.

FRIED TURKEY

WITH GIBLET GRAVY, MORTADELLA CORN BREAD DRESSING, AND CRANBERRY COMPOTE

Turkey, corn bread dressing, and gravy made from a turkey's giblet and neck bone were, and still are, a staple at our holiday tables and in the South. There is always someone looking to claim the legs and the wings. Fried turkey has become popular since the manufacturing of special turkey fryers, and the introduction of crowd-pleasing and deliciously fried turkey legs served at places like the North Carolina State Fair. Here, I use mortadella, an Italian sausage similar to bologna, to add a distinct, smoky-sweet flavor to the corn bread dressing. The turkey serves as the main dish in this holiday meal, while the corn bread dressing, cranberry sauce, and gravy are accompanying side dishes and condiments that complement the turkey.

NOTE: I like to fry my turkey on a stovetop. To make the turkey easier to handle and fry, the turkey is cut into 8 pieces, battered, and pan-fried, then the cooking is completed in the oven. This method produces a moist turkey on the inside with a nice crispness on the outside.

SERVES 8 TO 10

FOR THE TURKEY BRINE

1 turkey (10 to 12 pounds)
½ cup salt

FOR THE TURKEY

Vegetable oil for frying
4 cups milk
2 eggs, beaten
6 cups all-purpose flour
2 teaspoons salt
1½ teaspoons freshly ground black pepper

FOR THE GIBLET GRAVY

Turkey neck and giblets
1 large onion, cut in half
2 celery stalks
½ cup vegetable oil from the turkey fryer
2 cups all-purpose flour
Salt
Freshly ground black pepper

recipe continues →

TO BRINE THE TURKEY

Cut the turkey tail from the body, then cut along the backbone from the tail section to the neck. Cut along the breastbone from the neck to the tail. Next, cut the turkey into 8 pieces: 2 breast parts, 2 thigh parts, 2 legs, and 2 wings. Combine the salt and enough iced water to cover the turkey pieces in a large bowl. Brine the turkey overnight in the refrigerator.

TO FRY THE TURKEY

Preheat the oven to 350°F.

Pour enough vegetable oil into a deep fryer or large pot to cover the turkey pieces by ¼ inch. Heat the oil to 325°F. In a large bowl, mix together the milk and eggs. Dip the turkey pieces in the milk mixture and dredge them in the flour. Fry each piece on all sides until they are golden brown. Make sure not to overcrowd them. Drain them on paper towels, then place them in a single layer in a roasting pan. Roast until an instant-read thermometer inserted in the turkey pieces reaches 160° to 165°F. Remove the turkey pieces from the oven, drain them on paper towels, and pat off any excess oil. Reserve ¼ cup of the oil.

TO MAKE THE GIBLET GRAVY

While the turkey pieces are in the oven, make the gravy. Put the neck, giblets, onion, and celery in a large saucepan with enough water to cover them. Simmer for 1 hour. Remove the neck and giblets (reserve 2 cups of the water), and, when cool enough to handle, shred the meat from the neck and dice the giblets. Heat ¼ cup of the vegetable oil left over from frying the turkey in a saucepan. Stir in the flour over medium heat until the flour mixture becomes golden brown, 3 to 5 minutes. Whisk in the 2 cups of reserved cooking liquid from the giblets. Stir the mixture over medium heat until it is smooth. Add the neck and giblets meat, and salt and pepper to taste. Simmer for 10 minutes.

MORTADELLA CORN BREAD DRESSING

SERVES 8 TO 10

2 tablespoons unsalted butter
1 small onion, finely chopped
2 teaspoons of fresh sage or 1 teaspoon of dried sage
4 cups corn bread crumbs
½ French baguette, cut into cubes
1 cup finely chopped mortadella
½ cup grated Parmesan cheese
2 eggs, lightly beaten
2 cups water

Preheat the oven to 350°F.

In a small sauté pan over medium heat, melt the butter and sauté the onion and sage until the onion is translucent, about 5 minutes. Set aside to cool.

In a large bowl, combine the corn bread crumbs, bread cubes, mortadella, Parmesan cheese, eggs, water, and onion mixture. Spoon the mixture into a 2-quart baking dish. Bake until it is golden brown, 30 to 35 minutes.

CRANBERRY COMPOTE

MAKES ABOUT 3 CUPS

½ cup apple juice
¼ cup light brown sugar, packed
¼ teaspoon cinnamon
1 (12-ounce) package fresh cranberries
½ cup dried apricots, finely chopped
1 bay leaf

Put the apple juice, brown sugar, cinnamon, cranberries, apricots, and bay leaf in a medium saucepan. Stir over medium-high heat until the sugar dissolves and the mixture begins to boil. Reduce heat to low and simmer for 2 to 3 minutes until the cranberries burst.

Mortadella Corn Bread Dressing

Cranberry Compote

KOOL-AID IN A TEACUP

WHENEVER I PREPARE FOR a tea party, it conjures up memories of the beautiful 100-piece floral tea set my sisters and I received one Christmas as kids. We would invite each other and our neighboring friends to tea parties. The menu included milk, water, Kool-Aid, whatever was available in the refrigerator, and some of Mama's sugar cookies.

We set the dining table with our tea set and placed the cookies on a large platter in the center. We would sit around sipping the beverages from our teacups, taking cookies from the large platter, and placing them on our small china tea plates before we started to eat. We talked, laughed, and simply enjoyed our tea time together. Sometimes we would even sit on the front porch in a circle with empty cups and plates, pretending to be grown-ups and having just as much fun with our imaginary food and tea.

One of the most memorable adult tea sets from my childhood belonged to Mrs. Addie Robinson, the director of Holmes Daycare at Hargraves Community Center, where I attended preschool. She was a friend of my grand-

mother's, and she would invite my sisters Annette, Sandra, and me over for visits.

When I was eight years old, I got a chance to experience a traditional tea party at Mrs. Robinson's home. She had a white linen tablecloth on her oval table with matching tea napkins, china plates, cups, and saucers. This was all accompanied by a lovely silver tea set. In addition to the tea, there were sugar cubes served in a small crystal sugar bowl; thin, round slices of lemon neatly displayed on a floral etched plate; cucumber, chicken salad, and pimento cheese sandwiches; and lemon squares. She passed us cups of tea and served the food from a tiered plate stand.

Through the large window by our table, we had a beautiful view of her garden with its flowing fountain and rock pond. After tea, Mrs. Robinson would lead us outside to watch the goldfish swimming in the pond before we left. I loved going to her home, surrounded by beautiful things and a peaceful atmosphere.

I still enjoy tea time with my family and friends. I hope these recipes will inspire you to treat yourself and your loved ones to tea and quality time together more often.

CUCUMBER AND JALAPEÑO TEA SANDWICHES

The cooling flavor of cucumber goes well with the spiciness of jalapeño peppers, adding layers of flavors to the classic cucumber tea sandwich and bringing unexpected tastes to afternoon tea, as seen on the top tray on page 171.

SERVES 8

1 (8-ounce) package cream cheese, softened

1 medium cucumber, peeled, seeded, and finely diced

2 teaspoons grated onion

1 small jalapeño pepper, seeded and finely diced

½ teaspoon salt

½ teaspoon freshly ground black pepper

8 slices of thin-sliced white bread

In a medium bowl, combine all the ingredients except the bread and stir well. Spread the cucumber mixture equally onto 4 slices of bread. Top the sandwiches with the remaining 4 slices. Cut the crusts from the sandwiches and cut each sandwich into four equal slices.

Place a damp paper towel and plastic wrap over the sandwiches and refrigerate until needed.

ARUGULA AND EGG SALAD TEA SANDWICHES

Egg salad is a staple in the South. Serve these sandwiches for lunch or afternoon tea, as seen on the middle tray on page 171.

SERVES 8

- 6 extra large eggs, hard-boiled and grated
- ½ cup arugula, chopped
- ½ cup mayonnaise
- 2 tablespoons celery, finely chopped
- 1 tablespoon sweet pickle relish
- 1 teaspoon freshly ground black pepper
- ¼ teaspoon mustard
- ¼ teaspoon salt
- 8 slices of white or whole grain bread

In a medium bowl, combine all the ingredients except the bread and stir well. Refrigerate the egg salad for at least 2 hours. Spread the egg salad equally onto 4 slices of bread. Top the sandwiches with the remaining 4 slices. Cut the crusts from the sandwiches and cut each sandwich into four equal squares.

TOMATO AND SHRIMP BUTTER TEA SANDWICHES

Vine-ripened tomatoes layered between two slices of white bread spread with mayonnaise make the best tomato sandwiches. They are traditionally eaten during lunch, dinner, or on the fly from the abundance of the summer crop. Choose one extra-large tomato or two medium tomatoes to yield one pound. This recipe spruces up the humble tomato sandwich for a fashionable afternoon tea, as seen on the bottom tray on page 171.

SERVES 8

- ½ cup (1 stick) salted butter, softened
- 2 cups cooked, shelled, and deveined shrimp (about 12 ounces)
- 1 teaspoon finely grated lemon zest
- ¼ teaspoon freshly ground black pepper
- ¼ teaspoon granulated garlic
- 8 slices white bread, sliced thick
- 1 pound tomatoes (1 extra-large or 2 medium), sliced thin

In the bowl of a food processor fitted with a metal blade, add the butter, shrimp, lemon zest, black pepper, and garlic; process until the shrimp is ground.

Spread the shrimp butter equally onto 4 slices of the bread. Place tomato slices on top of the shrimp butter and top with another slice of bread. Trim the crust and cut each sandwich into four squares.

Place a damp paper towel and plastic wrap over sandwiches and refrigerate until needed.

GORGONZOLA AND WALNUT SCONES

These flaky, tender, and savory scones are delicious as is. You can also get creative with the finished scones and dress them up. Try them with a dollop of clotted cream and a drizzle of honey, or stuff them with savory treats like prosciutto or country ham.

MAKES 8 SCONES

- 2 cups all-purpose flour
- 1 tablespoon baking powder
- ⅛ teaspoon salt
- 2 tablespoons sugar
- 4 tablespoons unsalted butter, cold and cut into cubes
- ¼ cup Gorgonzola, crumbled and chilled (about 2 ounces)
- ½ cup heavy cream
- 2 eggs, beaten
- ½ cup walnuts, chopped

Preheat the oven to 425°F. Grease or line a baking sheet with parchment paper.

In a medium bowl, stir together the flour, baking powder, salt, and sugar. Using a pastry cutter or your fingertips, cut in the butter and Gorgonzola until pea-sized lumps form. In a separate bowl, whisk together the heavy cream and eggs. Pour the liquid mixture into the flour mixture and stir until the dough starts to come together. Add the walnuts and continue to stir until the dough comes together in a ball.

Place the dough on a lightly floured work surface. Dust a rolling pin with flour. Roll the dough into a ¾-inch-thick circle. Cut into 8 wedges with a floured knife or cut it into 10 rounds with a floured 2-inch cookie cutter. Arrange the wedges or rounds about 1 inch apart on the prepared baking sheet. Bake for 15 to 20 minutes, or until they are golden brown.

LEMON CURD

I like to serve this lemony recipe with scones and clotted cream for afternoon tea, as an ice cream topping, a dip for fresh fruit, or a swirl into yogurt. You will need three to four lemons to make ½ cup of lemon juice.

SERVES 12

- 5 egg yolks
- 1 cup sugar
- ½ cup fresh lemon juice
- 1 tablespoon finely grated lemon zest
- ½ cup (1 stick) unsalted butter, cold

In a heavy-bottomed medium saucepan, combine the egg yolks, sugar, and lemon juice. Cook the mixture over low heat, stirring until the mixture thickens and coats the back of a spoon. Stir in the lemon zest. Remove the mixture from the heat and stir in the butter, 2 tablespoons at a time. Pour the curd into a jar or container with an airtight lid. Let it cool to room temperature. Seal the filled jar and store it in the refrigerator to chill for at least 1 hour. Lemon curd can be stored in the refrigerator for up to 1 week.

DESSERTS

HOMEMADE CAKES

MAMA MADE HOMEMADE CAKES using a handheld mixer to prepare the batter in a large, white Pyrex bowl. Our job was to help her steady it while she beat enough air bubbles into the butter and sugar to make the mixture light and fluffy. Only then did the bowl stop wobbling from the mixer's rotating pressure. Sometimes, we would taste the butter-sugar mixture before it was fully creamed, feeling the grittiness of the sugar on our tongues and the slipperiness of the butter on the roofs of our mouths.

Once the butter-and-sugar mixture was well whipped, we each took turns cracking eggs into the bowl, one at a time, patiently waiting until Mama beat the batter well after each addition. Then, she sifted flour together with baking powder and salt. Finally, she added the dry ingredients alternately with the milk to the butter-sugar-egg mixture.

Observing the transformation from the floury sweetness of the raw cake batter to the browning of the sugar as it formed a golden crust, and the caramel and buttery smell of the cake baking in the oven, were all essential parts of oral recipe sharing.

The heightened aroma was our cue to check on the cake. A quick peep at the edge would tell us if it was pulling away from the sides of the pan. The true test, though, was Mama's gentle touch: Her handprint remaining on the surface meant the cake wasn't done, but when the surface sprang back when touched, the cake was ready to be removed from the oven. After Mama had frosted the cake, my sisters and I would divide up the bowl, spoon, and whisks and begin eating the frosting still clinging to their surfaces.

COCONUT CAKE
WITH COCONUT SOUR CREAM FROSTING

This recipe is for a classic yellow layer cake with a creamy coconut frosting. It was one of my favorite cakes that Mama made for dessert at Christmas.

SERVES 12

FOR THE CAKE

3 cups all-purpose flour
1 tablespoon baking powder
½ teaspoon salt
1 cup (2 sticks) unsalted butter, softened
2 cups sugar
3 eggs, at room temperature
1 cup unsweetened coconut milk
1 teaspoon vanilla extract

FOR THE COCONUT SOUR CREAM FROSTING

½ cup milk
½ cup unsweetened coconut milk
½ cup sour cream
1 cup sugar
1 tablespoon cornstarch
3 egg yolks
1 teaspoon vanilla extract
1 cup grated unsweetened coconut

TO MAKE THE CAKE

Preheat the oven to 350°F. Grease and flour two 9-inch round cake pans. In a medium bowl, sift together the flour, baking powder, and salt. In the bowl of an electric mixer fitted with the paddle attachment, cream the butter and sugar on medium speed until they are light and fluffy. Add the eggs one at a time, beating well after each addition, scraping down the bowl as needed.

Add the flour mixture to the butter mixture alternately with the coconut milk, in three additions, beginning and ending with the flour mixture, beating just until combined after each addition. Stir in the vanilla extract.

Pour the batter into the prepared cake pans and bake for 25 to 30 minutes, or until a toothpick inserted into the middle of the cake comes out clean. Let cool to room temperature before frosting.

TO MAKE THE COCONUT SOUR CREAM FROSTING

In a small heavy-bottomed saucepan, combine the milk, coconut milk, sour cream, sugar, cornstarch, and egg yolks. Cook the mixture over medium-low heat, stirring constantly until it is thickened, about 15 minutes. Stir in the vanilla extract and coconut. Let the frosting cool to room temperature and then place it in the refrigerator for 10 to 15 minutes, or until it is thick enough to spread.

Place one cake layer on a cake plate. Cover the top evenly with frosting. Top with the second cake layer and spread the remaining frosting over the sides and top.

Yellow Layer Cake
WITH PUMPKIN FROSTING

Mama began her first cookbook with the observation that her life was a lot like a pumpkin seed, and that, like a single pumpkin seed, her life could bring happiness and joy to others. The story inspired me to create this cake. I made it for Mama's 80th birthday celebration when we started Mama Dip's Share the Love Fund, established through the Triangle Community Foundation. It was a large pound cake layered with pumpkin frosting—big enough to feed 200 folks. This is the same recipe, but reduced to serve a dozen.

SERVES 12

FOR THE CAKE

2 cups all-purpose flour
2 teaspoons baking powder
¼ teaspoon salt
1 cup (2 sticks) unsalted butter, softened
1 cup sugar
5 eggs, separated
½ cup sour cream
2 teaspoons vanilla extract

FOR THE PUMPKIN FROSTING

1 pound confectioners' sugar
½ cup (1 stick) unsalted butter, softened
4 ounces cream cheese, softened
¼ cup mashed pumpkin, fresh or canned
2 teaspoons grated ginger
½ teaspoon vanilla extract

TO MAKE THE CAKE

Preheat the oven to 350°F. Grease and flour two 9-inch round cake pans.

In a bowl, sift together the flour, baking powder, and salt.

In the bowl of an electric mixer fitted with the paddle attachment, cream the butter and sugar on medium speed until they are light and fluffy. Add the egg yolks one at a time, beating well after each addition, scraping down the bowl as needed.

Add the flour mixture and sour cream in two additions, beginning and ending with the flour mixture, mixing on low until just combined. Stir in the vanilla extract. In the bowl of an electric mixer fitted with the whip attachment, beat the egg whites until soft peaks form. Gently fold the beaten egg whites into the batter.

Pour the batter into the prepared cake pans and bake the cake for 25 to 30 minutes, or until a toothpick inserted into the middle of the cake comes out clean. Let cool to room temperature before frosting.

TO MAKE THE PUMPKIN FROSTING

In a mixing bowl, combine the sugar, butter, cream cheese, pumpkin, ginger, and vanilla extract. Beat the mixture until it is light and fluffy.

TO ASSEMBLE

Place one cake layer on a cake plate. Cover the top evenly with frosting. Top with the second cake layer and spread the remaining frosting over the sides and top.

BANANA PUDDING

WITH CHOCOLATE MERINGUE

This recipe is inspired by Mama's special occasion dessert—layers of creamy vanilla custard, ripe bananas, and crisp wafers but with a little twist. While Mama topped hers with classic French meringue (those simple egg whites whipped with sugar, then broiled to golden perfection), I've added a hint of chocolate to that cloud-like topping. It's still made the same uncomplicated way she taught me—not heated sugar techniques, just that extra touch of chocolatey goodness. Ushering in a new generation of flavor to a classic dessert.

SERVES 8

FOR THE BANANA PUDDING

1 (11-ounce) box vanilla wafers
5 medium bananas
3 cups milk
5 egg yolks
½ cup sugar
5 tablespoons flour
2 tablespoons Myers's Rum

FOR THE CHOCOLATE MERINGUE

5 egg whites
¼ teaspoon cream of tartar
½ cup sugar
2 tablespoons cocoa powder

TO MAKE THE BANANA PUDDING

In a 9-inch baking dish, layer the vanilla wafers and slice the bananas over the wafers, starting and ending with the wafers. Set aside.

In a saucepan, whisk together the milk, egg yolks, sugar, flour, and rum. Cook the mixture over medium-low heat until it is thickened, 6 to 8 minutes.

Pour the mixture evenly over the layered wafers and bananas. Let it cool slightly.

TO MAKE THE CHOCOLATE MERINGUE

In a stand mixer fitted with a wire whisk, beat the egg whites and cream of tartar on high speed until they are frothy. Gradually add the sugar and continue beating the mixture until stiff peaks form. Fold in the cocoa powder.

TO ASSEMBLE AND BAKE

Preheat the oven to 375°F.

Spread the meringue evenly over the top of the banana pudding. Place the dish in the oven and bake for 8 to 10 minutes, or until the meringue is toasted.

APPLE CRISP

WITH CINNAMON WHIPPED CREAM

Besides the apples we picked from trees in neighbors' backyards, there was plenty to pick and gather from the ground at a family friend's home in the countryside, where there was a small apple orchard. Apple crisp was a quicker dessert to make than an apple pie or cobbler, and that is why Mama would make it for a special Saturday dessert after we had peeled the apples for her to make apple butter and apple preserves.

SERVES 6

FOR THE APPLE CRISP

- 6 medium Granny Smith apples, peeled, cored, and thinly sliced
- ½ cup raisins
- 1 tablespoon lemon juice
- 2 tablespoons apple brandy
- 1 teaspoon cinnamon
- ½ cup water
- ½ cup granulated sugar
- ½ cup light brown sugar, packed
- ½ cup all-purpose flour
- ½ cup rolled oats
- ½ cup (1 stick) unsalted butter, cold

FOR THE CINNAMON WHIPPED CREAM

- 2 tablespoons confectioners' sugar
- ¼ teaspoon cinnamon
- 1 cup heavy cream, chilled
- ½ teaspoon vanilla extract

TO MAKE THE APPLE CRISP

Preheat the oven to 350°F.

In a large bowl, combine the apples, raisins, lemon juice, brandy, cinnamon, and water and toss together to coat the apples. Arrange the apple mixture in an 8-inch square baking dish. Combine the granulated sugar, brown sugar, flour, and oats in a small bowl. Cut in the butter with your fingers or a fork until the mixture forms coarse crumbs. Sprinkle the mixture evenly over the apples.

Bake for 35 to 40 minutes, or until the apples are tender and the topping is golden brown. Remove from the oven and let cool slightly. Serve with Cinnamon Whipped Cream on the side.

TO MAKE THE CINNAMON WHIPPED CREAM

Combine the sugar and cinnamon in a small bowl. Add the heavy cream to a medium bowl and beat with a hand mixer on high speed until foamy. Gradually add the cinnamon sugar and vanilla and beat until soft peaks form. Keep chilled until ready to use.

STRAWBERRY BISCUIT CAKE

This delicious biscuit cake is full of flavor. Serve this wonderful dessert with whipped cream or ice cream and a glass of champagne for a beautiful end to a meal.

SERVES 6 TO 8

- 1⅔ cups self-rising flour
- ½ teaspoon baking powder
- ¼ teaspoon salt
- ½ cup plus 3 tablespoons sugar
- 1 teaspoon cinnamon
- 4 tablespoons unsalted butter, cold
- ¼ cup heavy cream
- 1 egg
- 1 cup sour cream
- 1 tablespoon all-purpose flour
- 1 pint fresh strawberries, hulled and sliced
- ¼ cup pistachios, chopped

Preheat the oven to 375°F. Butter a 9-inch round cake pan. Set aside.

In a large bowl, mix together the self-rising flour, baking powder, salt, 3 tablespoons of the sugar, and cinnamon. Cut in the butter with a fork or pastry cutter until the mixture resembles coarse crumbs. Make a well in the center. Add the heavy cream and egg and stir until a soft dough forms. Press the dough evenly into the prepared baking pan.

In a medium bowl, combine the sour cream, all-purpose flour, and the remaining ½ cup of sugar. Stir until the sugar dissolves. Fold the strawberries into the mixture. Spoon it evenly over the biscuit dough.

Bake for 55 to 60 minutes, or until it is firm in the center and golden brown. Sprinkle the pistachios evenly over the cake.

GOAT CHEESE POUND CAKE

Mrs. Annie Mae Mason was a family friend and known throughout our community for her artisan skill for making homemade butter. She was the only person in our community who I knew of who still churned cream. Her delicious pound cakes using her homemade butter made me want to re-create the flavor, so I added goat cheese to this pound cake recipe as a tribute to her flavorful pound cake.

SERVES 12

- 3 cups all-purpose flour
- 1 teaspoon baking powder
- ¾ pound (3 sticks) unsalted butter, softened
- 1 (4-ounce) package goat cheese, softened
- 2½ cups sugar
- 5 eggs
- 2 teaspoons fresh lemon juice

Preheat the oven to 325°F.

Grease and flour a pound cake or Bundt pan. In a medium bowl, sift together the flour and baking powder; set aside. In the bowl of a stand mixer fitted with the paddle attachment, cream together the butter and goat cheese on medium speed until fluffy. Gradually add the sugar, and beat until light and fluffy. Add the eggs one at a time, beating for 1 minute after each addition. Scrape down the bowl and beat for 1 minute. Add the flour mixture 1 cup at a time and mix on low speed until incorporated. Stir in the lemon juice. Pour the batter into the prepared pan and spread evenly.

Bake in a preheated oven for 1 to 1½ hours, until golden brown, or until a toothpick inserted into the middle of the cake comes out clean. Let the cake cool for 10 minutes before removing it from the pan.

IT TAKES A VILLAGE

TWO WOMEN IN MY community left an unforgettable mark on my memory. Like many of the other parents and grandparents in our community, these two women created a nurturing environment for the children—sitting on their front porches, watching us play, offering lemonade or Kool-Aid, and serving a dip or two of hand-cranked ice cream. They did not command respect; instead, they received respect through their caring spirits. But what set these two women apart was their attachment to their wood-burning, cast-iron stoves. There was even a time when I dreamt of owning a cast-iron stove. I found one, but did not buy it because I did not have space in my kitchen, nor did I have space outside for it. Still, I found pleasure in the hunt, and it was a nostalgic thing to do.

MRS. ANNIE MAE MASON

HER SIZABLE, ACTIVE KITCHEN had two stoves: a modern electric one and her favorite, a wood-burning stove. Mrs. Mason was well known in our community for her sweet, buttery, tangy pound cakes, made using her homemade butter churned in an old-fashioned stoneware churn. She also used fresh whipping cream from grass-fed cows. The cream was delivered right to her door from a local dairy farm. On occasion, Mama would send me to Mrs. Mason's home to pick up a pound or two of her butter.

I was always happy to make the 15-minute journey westward to her home in Carrboro, crossing two neighborhoods and two creeks. I'd take time out to greet folks at their homes as I walked down their street. Using rocks as my stepping stones, I crossed the second creek—a shorter crossing than the creek nearer to my home. After stepping out of the small wooded area into the sunshine, I walked along Broad Street toward her house. There, the artistically designed topiaries in her front yard came into full view, delightful box hedges shaped like birds, squirrels, and other animals, all connected by a hedge arch at the entrance. Once inside, the hedges were shaped like a bench next to their rose garden. Mrs. Mason's husband, Mr. Morris Mason, was the architect of their beautiful garden, and he kept it well manicured.

As I stood and knocked on Mrs. Mason's front screen door, watching for her to appear in the hallway leading to her kitchen, the tangy, buttery aroma of pound cake baking hit my nostrils. She would always welcome me in to sit at her butcher-block kitchen table for a chat, sharing her collection of tableware as we talked about our shared love for baking. During the winter months, she used her wood-burning stove, adjusting its dampers and vents to keep the fire burning at the desired temperature for cooking while enjoying the warmth of her kitchen.

Depending on the time of year, she asked how I was doing in school or how my summer was going, and encouraged me to be a good girl. A slice of her homemade pound cake was an added bonus to my visits. Its distinctive flavor was different from the pound cakes made from store-bought butter, imparting a tangy taste and rich aroma. I knew the butter had to be unique for Mama to send me all the way to Mrs. Mason's home. I was touched that she shared an ancestral technique with me, handed down from her mother's mother, and by the loving care she showed as she gently wrapped wax paper around the butter for me to carry back to Mama.

MRS. ANNIE PEARL MCCLELLAND

THE SECOND WOOD-BURNING STOVE that I encountered in our community belonged to our next-door neighbor, Mrs. Annie Pearl McClelland. On a summer afternoon, out of the blue, she stepped outside with her ruffled apron tied around her waist and called out to get our attention. She had an inclination to assemble us—a few neighborhood girls playing outside—for a fish fry. She had been fishing and wanted us to share in the cooking of the meal in her yard. Her black, cast-iron, wood-burning stove stood in the side yard next to her house, ready to be fired up.

Mrs. Annie Pearl asked each of us to gather ingredients from our home kitchens: "You bring the two cups of flour, you bring the four eggs, and you go to your house and bring some milk." We ran swiftly to our homes like kids who had to be indoors before the streetlights came on, eager to bring back what she had asked for.

After returning with our ingredients, we sat at Mrs. Annie Pearl's rustic table on a bench made of plywood and cinder blocks that sagged in the middle as we watched her prepare the meal. She started a fire in her stove, first using twigs and small branches and then adding larger logs once the branches were well lit. One by one, she dipped each fish into a pan of salted water, then coated it with cornmeal. We watched the bubbling hot oil in her cast-iron skillet and heard the snap, crackle, and pop sounds when she placed the cornmeal-coated fish in it. We marveled at the toasted smell of cornmeal and the aroma of the fresh porgies frying.

Next, she combined flour, sugar, baking powder, and salt in a large bowl before adding milk, eggs, and melted butter, stirring until the mixture was smooth. She poured the batter into another cast-iron skillet greased with lard and then placed it in the oven to bake. When she opened the oven to check for doneness, the sweet-smelling bouquet caused me to ask, "Mrs. Annie Pearl, what is that?"

She replied, "Sweet bread. My sweet bread."

It was still piping hot when we each received a piece, topped with a lump of butter that melted into the sliced edges of the bread.

She peeled and thinly sliced potatoes and onions, then placed them in a hot skillet with melted lard. She cooked them over high heat until they were crispy and brown. She then poured off the oil, added a sprinkling of salt, and slid the pan onto the stovetop where the flames were lower, and continued to cook until the interior of the potatoes were fluffy.

Once she had finished cooking, we set the table with pie tin plates, forks, paper napkins, and a mason jar of wildflowers we had gathered from the wooded area of her backyard. The porgies were crispy on the outside, flaky and moist on the inside, and tasted like they were just caught from the waters. The sweet bread was mouthwatering. Creamy coleslaw completed the meal.

We were grateful for the delicious meal Mrs. Annie Pearl prepared for us, feeding us and keeping us company during the summer months while we were on break from school and our parents were at work. Even now, when I make sweet bread, it brings back the sweet, buttery aroma that I smelled when Mrs. Annie Pearl used a dish towel to pull on the hot handle of the cast-iron oven door and slid out her prized loaf.

SWEET BREAD
WITH RASPBERRIES

I will never forget the first time I tasted this simple quick bread, savoring it as a dessert under a shade tree on a warm summer afternoon. The memory of that moment has stayed with me, inspiring me to enhance the recipe with juicy raspberries. Now, each bite offers bursts of tangy sweetness, combining cherished memories with a fresh, fruity twist.

SERVES 6

2 cups all-purpose flour
1 cup sugar
2 teaspoons baking powder
½ teaspoon salt
1 cup milk
2 eggs, well beaten
6 tablespoons unsalted butter, melted
Finely grated zest of 1 lemon
1 (6-ounce) package fresh raspberries

Preheat the oven to 350°F.

Grease and flour a loaf pan. In a large bowl, mix together the flour, sugar, baking powder, and salt. In a separate bowl, mix the milk, eggs, butter, and lemon zest and stir to combine. Pour the wet ingredients into the dry ingredients and stir until just combined. Gently fold in the fresh raspberries, being careful not to crush them. Pour into the prepared pan. Bake for 50 to 60 minutes until golden brown.

SWEET POTATO AND PECAN PIE

Just like my grandmother's sweet potato pie, this dessert uses baked sweet potatoes to achieve that perfect caramel sweetness, complemented by the buttery crunch of pecans. This special combination brings back cherished memories of foraging for pecans and of the clouds of flavor coming from my grandmother's kitchen. Bringing these two treasured memories together produces a slice of comfort that connects the past to our present celebrations. To create a chocolate version, add one cup of chocolate chips to the recipe along with the pecans.

SERVES 8

1 medium sweet potato
1 unbaked pie shell
½ cup light brown sugar, packed
½ cup granulated sugar
½ cup (1 stick) unsalted butter, melted
2 eggs, well beaten
1 cup chopped pecans
1 cup chocolate chips (optional)

Preheat the oven to 350°F.

Bake the sweet potato until it is tender but not soft, about 30 minutes. Let the sweet potato cool, remove the peel, and slice it into rounds. Lay the rounds evenly in the pie shell.

In a medium bowl, whisk together the brown sugar, granulated sugar, butter, and eggs. Stir in the pecans and chocolate chips (if using). Pour the mixture over the sweet potato–filled pie shell. Bake the pie for 50 to 60 minutes, or until the filling is set.

FRESH FRUIT PINEAPPLE UPSIDE-DOWN CAKE

I purchase a pineapple for two reasons: to use as decor on my kitchen counter or to add to my fruit bowl. When cherry season is in full bloom, I like to use fresh cherries to make this pineapple upside-down cake, one of my favorite desserts.

SERVES 8

FOR THE TOPPING

- 4 tablespoons unsalted butter
- 1 cup light brown sugar, packed
- 10 large cherries, pitted and sliced in half
- 2 cups chopped fresh pineapple (1 small pineapple)

FOR THE CAKE

- 1⅔ cups all-purpose flour
- 2 teaspoons baking powder
- ½ teaspoon salt
- ½ cup (1 stick) unsalted butter, softened
- ¾ cup sugar
- 2 large eggs
- ½ cup milk
- ½ teaspoon vanilla extract

TO MAKE THE TOPPING

Grease the bottom and sides of a 9-inch square baking pan. Melt the butter over low heat in a small pot. Add the brown sugar and stir until the sugar melts. Pour the mixture into the prepared baking pan and spread evenly. Arrange the cherries over the sugar mixture. Arrange the pineapple over the cherries.

TO MAKE THE CAKE

Preheat the oven to 350°F.

Whisk the flour, baking powder, and salt together in a medium bowl. Cream the butter with an electric mixer at medium speed in a large bowl. Gradually add the sugar and continue beating until light and fluffy. Add the eggs one at a time, beating well after each addition. Add the flour mixture alternately with the milk, beginning and ending with flour. Stir in the vanilla.

Pour the batter evenly over the fruit and bake for 50 to 60 minutes, or until a toothpick inserted in the center comes out clean. Remove the cake from the oven and let cool for 20 minutes. Run a butter knife or offset spatula around the edge and invert onto a cake plate.

OATMEAL PEANUT BUTTER BARS

This is a recipe I created by accident when I forgot to include the eggs when making oatmeal cookies. Rather than throwing out the batter, I improvised and created these oatmeal bars layered with peanut butter and chocolate. I shared them with our staff at Mama Dip's Kitchen. Tommy, one of our line cooks, loved them so much that on occasion he would ask me with his Southern-slang dialect whether I had any more of those "peanut butter thangs."

SERVES 8

- 1½ cups all-purpose flour
- 1 teaspoon baking soda
- ¼ teaspoon salt
- 1 cup brown sugar
- ½ cup granulated sugar
- ½ cup (1 stick) unsalted butter
- 3 cups quick-cooking oats
- 1 teaspoon vanilla extract
- 1 cup peanut butter
- 1 cup chocolate chips

Preheat the oven to 350°F.

Combine the flour, baking soda, and salt in a small bowl.

In a stand mixer bowl fitted with a paddle, beat the brown sugar, granulated sugar, and butter until they are light and fluffy. Stir in the flour mixture. Increase the speed and beat to combine. Stir in the oats and vanilla until they are combined.

Press half of the dough into the bottom of an 8-inch square baking pan. Spread the peanut butter evenly over the top of the dish. Sprinkle the chocolate chips over the peanut butter. Add the remaining dough and press it evenly to the edge.

Bake for 25 to 30 minutes. Allow to cool completely to room temperature before cutting.

GOOD PEOPLE

AMONG ALL THE SHOPKEEPERS in the neighborhood, Edward G. Danziger, affectionately known as Papa D., stood out with his warm welcome. He was the proprietor of Danziger's Old World Candy Shop, which later grew into Danziger's Old World Restaurant. The next generation of Danzigers opened the Zoom Zoom and Rathskeller restaurants. Located on Franklin Street in the heart of downtown Chapel Hill, Danziger's was a whole new ball game. They did not mind Black customers in their store.

The Danzigers were immigrants of the Jewish faith who left behind a successful candy factory in Vienna and five stores throughout Europe. They fled Austria to escape the threat of the concentration camps, moved to Chapel Hill, received a grant from the Quaker faith community, and started their highly successful businesses. In a time when segregation was still the unspoken rule of many establishments, the Danzigers welcomed Black customers and hired Black employees to wait tables and manage their businesses, despite the pushback they received.

My sisters and I would mostly go to their candy shop on Sundays after church. It was different from any place I had ever entered, with its two-seat round tables and decorous atmosphere that made you want to dress up before entering. The ladies behind the counter wore dresses, skirts, blouses, and heeled shoes, which made me feel like I was entering a special place.

Before my memorable Sunday trips to Danziger's, I was a frequent customer at our neighborhood corner store, which sold a wide assortment of novelty candies. I enjoyed their two-for-five-cents pieces of candy and gum, such as Pixy Stix, candy necklaces, chewing gum shaped like cigarettes that released a puff of powder, and Gold Nugget gum in tiny cloth sacks with a yellow drawstring. There was Bazooka bubble gum, hard as a rock until it softened into an excellent chew that you could then blow the best bubbles; and as a bonus, each piece was wrapped with a Bazooka Joe comic strip printed on wax paper. Laffy Taffy banana candy, Fruit Stripe gum, red Wax Lips, caramel Sugar Babies, Tootsie Pops with a fudge center, oversized Tootsie Rolls, Red Hot balls, and spicy Cinnamon Hearts were my standard purchases during the week.

But Sundays were different. On Sundays, it was time for something unique.

Inside Danziger's Old World Candy Shop, I fell in love at first sight—with a milk chocolate–coated tasty wonder sitting on a platter in a crystal-clear display case. It was shiny, smooth, and layered with rich, sweet, buttery caramel and crunchy pecan halves, and called a chocolate turtle because of its shape.

On a shelf below, I saw two confections displayed that made me wonderstruck. It was my first time seeing or hearing of rock candy and white chocolate. The rock candy, with its pure sugary flavor, crunchy texture, and crystal-clear pale color, was made so you could see the string that it was attached to. That string of goodness looked back at me with a glaring wink. It had a hold on me. I had to hold back my enthusiasm each time I waited my turn to order because I did not want to lose my patience while waiting in line. But after I had eaten the rock candy, I gave the string a good chew to release the sugariness that had soaked into the string onto my taste buds. White chocolate was another first. Its buttery, creamy, and vanilla flavors at the first bite reminded me of vanilla ice cream.

When we finished our purchase at Danziger's, it was time to walk home toward the west end of Franklin Street. We made a medley for our short trip home, composed of strolling, skipping, and playing invisible hopscotch, happy to have been in the company of "good people"—folks with good character.

CHOCOLATE CAKE

WITH CARAMEL PECAN FUDGE FROSTING

This moist and heavenly chocolate cake is a tribute to my first chocolate turtle, and is inspired by the rich flavors and textures of pecan nut clusters. It also honors my memory of being welcomed into Danziger's Old World Candy Shop.

SERVES 12

FOR THE CAKE

2 cups all-purpose flour

⅔ cup cocoa

2 tablespoons cornstarch

1 teaspoon baking soda

½ teaspoon baking powder

½ teaspoon salt

¾ cup (1½ sticks) unsalted butter, softened

1¾ cups sugar

3 eggs, separated

1 cup plus 2 tablespoons buttermilk

1 teaspoon vanilla extract

FOR THE CARAMEL PECAN FUDGE FROSTING

⅔ cup unsalted butter

¼ cup cocoa

1 cup light brown sugar, packed

½ cup half-and-half

1 cup pecan pieces

3 cups confectioners' sugar

TO MAKE THE CAKE

Preheat the oven to 350°F. Grease and flour two 9-inch round cake pans.

In a medium bowl, sift together the flour, cocoa, cornstarch, baking soda, baking powder, and salt. In the bowl of an electric mixer fitted with the paddle attachment, cream together the butter and sugar until they are light and fluffy. Add the egg yolks one at a time, beating well after each addition, scraping down the bowl as needed. Add the flour mixture alternately with the buttermilk, in three additions, beginning and ending with the flour mixture.

In another medium bowl, beat the egg whites until stiff with a hand mixer and fold into the cake batter. Stir in the vanilla. Divide the batter between the prepared cake pans and bake for 25 to 30 minutes, until golden brown and when a toothpick inserted into the center comes out clean. Let the cake cool for a few minutes and then remove from the pans. Allow the cake to cool to room temperature before frosting.

TO MAKE THE CARAMEL PECAN FUDGE FROSTING

Preheat the oven to 325°F.

Melt the butter in a medium saucepan over low heat and stir in the cocoa until well combined. Add the brown sugar and cook for 2 minutes, stirring constantly. Add the half-and-half and increase the heat to medium. Cook, stirring until the mixture boils. Remove from the heat and let cool to room temperature.

While waiting for the frosting to cool, place the pecans on a baking sheet and toast in a preheated 325°F oven for 3 to 5 minutes and let cool. Coarsely chop the pecans; set aside. Put the confectioners' sugar in the bowl of a stand mixer fitted with a paddle. Add the cooled caramel mixture and beat on medium speed until the frosting is smooth and fluffy.

TO ASSEMBLE

Once the cake cools to room temperature, place one cake layer on a cake plate. With a spatula, evenly spread one cup of frosting to cover the layer. Top with the second layer and spread the remaining frosting all over the sides and top of the cake. Sprinkle the toasted pecans over the top of the frosted cake.

CHOCOLATE BREAD PUDDING

WITH CANDIED BACON

This recipe brings together three pairings: chocolate and bourbon, bacon and bourbon, and maple syrup and bourbon. I should call this recipe bourbon food pairings, but it's actually a not-so-classic Southern bread pudding. The bourbon adds oaky, vanilla, caramel, and spice flavors. The savory flavor comes from the topping of maple and black pepper candied bacon. I like to serve it warm with vanilla ice cream.

SERVES 6 TO 8

FOR THE BREAD PUDDING

2 cups soft bread crumbs
¼ cup sugar
¼ cup cocoa
2 teaspoons baking powder
3 cups milk
3 eggs, beaten
4 tablespoons unsalted butter, melted
¼ cup bourbon
1 teaspoon vanilla extract
1 cup chocolate chips

FOR THE CANDIED BACON

¼ cup brown sugar
2 teaspoons black pepper, freshly ground
6 strips of applewood smoked bacon
2 tablespoons maple syrup

TO MAKE THE BREAD PUDDING

Preheat the oven to 350°F.

In a large bowl, mix together the bread crumbs, sugar, cocoa, and baking powder.

In another bowl, whisk together the milk, eggs, butter, bourbon, and vanilla. Stir the milk mixture and chocolate chips into the bread crumb mixture. Pour the pudding into a buttered 1-quart casserole dish. Bake the dish for 50 to 60 minutes, or until a knife inserted in the center comes out clean.

TO MAKE THE CANDIED BACON

Preheat the oven to 375°F. Line a rimmed cookie sheet with aluminum foil. Set a cooling rack on top of the foil.

In a bowl, mix together the brown sugar and pepper. Brush both sides of the bacon strips with the maple syrup and arrange them on the cooling rack. Sprinkle the sugar mixture evenly over the top sides of the bacon.

Bake for 15 to 20 minutes, or until done. Cool the bacon, cut into small pieces, and sprinkle over the pudding.

LEMON CHESS PIE
WITH CARDAMOM

Chess pie is made with eggs, sugar, and butter with just enough cornmeal and flour to create the contrast between the delicately crisp top and a smooth custard beneath. I've added cardamom here, one of my favorite spices from India. Cardamom's warm floral notes balance the pie's sweetness and add just enough spiciness to make memories around your family table even sweeter.

SERVES 8

- 1 tablespoon all-purpose flour
- 1 tablespoon white cornmeal
- 1½ cups sugar
- 2 teaspoons ground cardamom
- 4 eggs
- ⅓ cup half-and-half
- 4 tablespoons unsalted butter, melted
- ¼ cup fresh lemon juice
- 2 teaspoons finely grated lemon zest
- 1 unbaked pie shell

Preheat the oven to 325°F.

Combine the flour, cornmeal, sugar, and cardamom in a medium bowl. Beat together the eggs, half-and-half, butter, lemon juice, and lemon zest in a medium bowl. Add the wet mixture to the flour mixture and stir to combine.

Pour the batter into the unbaked pie shell. Bake the pie for 45 to 50 minutes, or until a knife inserted in the middle comes out clean.

ICE CREAM

LONG MEADOW FARM DAIRY STORE, also known as the Dairy Bar, was a treasure trove of once-forbidden flavors, located on the west end of Franklin Street, just three blocks from my home. Before I ever stepped inside, my experience with store-brought ice cream had been limited to the tasty but prepackaged treats found in corner store freezers: ice cream cups, toffee crunch bars, Creamsicles, ice cream sandwiches, Nutty Buddys, Push-Up pops, and Popsicles. The arrival of the ice cream truck, signaled by its familiar melodies, sent us kids in the neighborhood running to our parents for money to buy its delicious soft-serve ice cream on a cake cone. No one could top Mama's recipes for homemade snow cream, or her hand-churned ice cream made with a hand-crank machine, but they were saved for summer cookouts and birthday parties. But the Dairy Bar promised a new collection of flavors and textures and a delicious diversity of ice cream.

After desegregation, Saturday afternoons at the ice cream parlor became my time for adventure. Oh, what a promotion and feast for the senses! The sound of milkshakes churning in stainless steel containers and the aroma of toasted grilled cheese sandwiches kept me coming back for more. One could peep at the stainless steel machines that produced ice cream made in-house, while the swinging door to the kitchen flapped as a worker passed through. The ice cream flavors included black cherry, butter pecan, rocky road, lemon custard, orange sherbet, chocolate chip, fudge ripple, banana, vanilla, and many more.

Civil rights demonstrators in front of Long Meadow Dairy Store, February 1960.

The Dairy Bar's ice cream concoctions were the crème de la crème. Banana splits arrived in oblong glass banana split boats. Hot fudge sundaes sat nestled in footed tulip-shaped glasses. Ice cream sundaes with three scoops and layers of fruit fillings were packed in big, tall glasses, and served with an extra-long spoon to reach the chocolate syrup resting on the bottom. The attendant would decorate each ice cream sundae, banana split, and milkshake with a variety of toppings—fruit sauces, chocolate sauce, and walnuts in syrup—then top it off with a generous dollop of whipped cream and a cherry.

Sometimes, I sat at a booth by the window and looked out onto Franklin Street—it was like a little oasis in the middle of a bustling town. Or I would sit in a cozy booth near the counter and watch as the attendant prepared my favorite order—crispy french fries, a grilled cheese sandwich made with American cheese oozing out of the center of the diagonal slices, and a vanilla milkshake.

The Dairy Bar became a cornerstone of Mama's party planning. The self-service freezer held neatly packed bricks of Neapolitan ice cream—vanilla, chocolate, and strawberry—ready for any gathering. Individual servings of vanilla and chocolate ice cream—complete with a wooden spoon and the perfect size to serve to kids at community socials—were always available, and sold by the dozen.

Each visit to the Dairy Bar was an adventure—a sweet taste of freedom on the west end of Franklin Street. It stood as a symbol of change and progress—a place where I felt comfortable and could sit and enjoy something delicious just a hop, skip, and jump from my home. Inspired by those memories, I created my own ice cream recipes, sharing the same joy and indulgence I once found at the Dairy Bar with my own family and friends.

SWEET POTATO CUSTARD ICE CREAM

Mama's homemade ice cream was a special treat at our cookout parties during the summer months. Each kid would have a chance to turn the old-fashioned hand crank until the ice cream became too hard for the little ones, and then the adults would take over. This custard recipe has added flavor from the baked sweet potatoes and a surprise crunch of lemon flavor from the lemon drops. Make sure to crush the candy to eliminate any large chunks.

SERVES 8

3 cups milk
1 cup heavy cream
5 egg yolks, slightly stirred
½ cup sugar
¼ teaspoon cinnamon
1 teaspoon vanilla extract
1 cup mashed baked sweet potatoes
½ cup lemon drop candy, crushed

In a medium saucepan over medium heat, scald the milk and cream. In a small bowl, whisk ¼ cup of the scalded milk mixture into the slightly stirred egg yolks until combined. While whisking, pour the scalded milk and egg yolk mixture into the remaining milk mixture, along with the sugar. Whisk together until the sugar dissolves. Cook over medium-low heat, stirring constantly with a wooden spoon until the mixture thickens and coats the back of the spoon, 8 to 10 minutes. To check to see if it's ready, trace a finger across the back of the spoon. It will leave a trail if the custard is ready.

Remove the custard from the heat. Stir in the cinnamon, vanilla, and sweet potatoes. Cool the mixture to room temperature and then chill it in the refrigerator for at least 2 hours. Freeze in an ice cream maker according to the manufacturer's directions. Add the crushed lemon drops in the last few minutes of churning. Spoon the ice cream into an airtight container and place it in the freezer for at least 1 hour before serving.

GINGER SNAP ICE CREAM

This ice cream gets most of its sweetness and flavor from the molasses, plus a nice burst of flavor from the candied ginger.

SERVES 8

- 2 cups heavy cream
- 2 cups half-and-half
- ½ cup molasses
- ¼ cup sugar
- 1 teaspoon cinnamon
- ¼ teaspoon cloves
- 1 teaspoon vanilla extract
- ½ cup candied ginger, finely chopped

In a medium saucepan over medium heat, combine the cream, half-and-half, molasses, sugar, cinnamon, and cloves. Stir until well mixed and the sugar is dissolved. Cook over medium-low heat, stirring constantly with a wooden spoon until the mixture thickens and coats the back of the spoon, 8 to 10 minutes. Remove from the heat and stir in the vanilla. Cool the mixture to room temperature, cover, and chill in the refrigerator for at least 2 hours.

Freeze the mixture in an ice cream maker according to the manufacturer's directions. Add the candied ginger in the last few minutes of churning. Spoon the ice cream into an airtight container and place it in the freezer for at least 1 hour before serving.

CANTALOUPE AND RASPBERRY MILKSHAKE

I first started with a cantaloupe milkshake, taking as its inspiration a simple dessert my mother served of a cantaloupe wedge topped with scoops of vanilla ice cream at Mama Dip's Kitchen. Then, I decided to add raspberries because of the color contrast and tart flavor of the raspberries. The sweet, juicy cantaloupe is complemented by the tart raspberries, creating a refreshing treat. Serve it at your next summer gathering and wait for the *hums* and *yums*.

MAKES 1 MILKSHAKE

- 3 large scoops vanilla ice cream
- 1 cup chopped cantaloupe, chilled
- ½ cup raspberries
- 1 teaspoon sugar

In a blender, combine the ice cream, cantaloupe, raspberries, and sugar. Blend until smooth and creamy.

PEACH AND CITRUS ICE CREAM

This refreshing ice cream combines the sweetness of ripe peaches with a creamy base, and the lemon and orange zests add a bright tang that perfectly complements the fruit's natural flavor.

SERVES 8

2 cups half-and-half
1 cup milk
5 egg yolks, slightly beaten
1¼ cups sugar
1 pound peaches
Finely grated zest of 1 lemon
Finely grated zest of 1 orange

In a medium saucepan, scald the half-and-half and milk over low heat. In a small bowl, whisk ¼ cup of the scalded milk mixture into the slightly beaten egg yolks until combined. While whisking, pour the scalded milk and egg yolk mixture into the remaining milk mixture, along with the sugar. Whisk together until the sugar dissolves. Cook over medium-low heat, stirring constantly with a wooden spoon until the mixture thickens and coats the back of the spoon, 8 to 10 minutes. To check to see if it's ready, trace a finger across the back of the spoon. It will leave a trail if the custard is ready.

Remove from the heat and let cool to room temperature. Lightly score an X on the bottom of each peach. Blanch the peaches in a pot of boiling water for 60 seconds. Remove the peaches with a spoon and place them in a bowl of ice water for a few seconds. Peel and pit the peaches. Purée the peaches in a food processor or blender. Stir the cream mixture with the peach purée, lemon zest, and orange zest. Pour into a large container, cover and chill in the refrigerator for 2 hours or overnight. Freeze in an ice cream maker according to the manufacturer's directions.

ORANGE CREAM PUNCH

Having this punch as part of dessert at our birthday parties was a family tradition that my mother started. The punch bowl, filled with this delightful concoction, was brought to the table just before our birthday cakes. You can make individual servings by placing one scoop of ice cream and one scoop of sherbet in an individual glass or bowl and topping with ginger ale.

SERVES 8 TO 10

- 1 quart vanilla ice cream
- 1 quart orange sherbet
- 1 (16-ounce) bottle ginger ale, chilled

Scoop the ice cream and sherbet into a punch bowl. Slowly pour the ginger ale over the scoops of ice cream and sherbet. Serve immediately.

DRINKS

OLD-FASHIONED LEMONADE

Sipping a glass of homemade lemonade brings me back to when I was a young girl sitting on the front porch on a summer Saturday evening, waiting on the call from Mama in the backyard that the cookout food was ready to be served. This simple lemonade is made without a simple syrup; the acid in the lemons and warm water dissolve the sugar. I like to keep lemonade on hand for a quick beverage and to make the Chapel Hill Cocktail (page 229).

SERVES 6

- 2 cups fresh lemon juice (about 12 lemons)
- 2 cups sugar
- 8 cups warm water

Combine the lemon juice and sugar in a large pitcher and stir for 1 minute. Add the water and stir until the sugar dissolves. Serve chilled.

CARDAMOM ICED TEA

Sip this refreshing tea in a tall glass on those days when you want to sit on the porch and smell the roses or you need an afternoon boost of energy. I use Earl Grey, a blend of black tea from India and Ceylon, to make this iced tea.

SERVES 4

½ cup loose black tea or 8 tea bags
3 cups cold water
6 cardamom pods, crushed
1 teaspoon ground ginger
1 teaspoon cinnamon
¼ teaspoon freshly ground black pepper
½ cup sugar
¾ cup evaporated milk
Ice

Place the loose tea in a tea ball.

Add the water to a small pot, along with the cardamom, ginger, cinnamon, and pepper. Stir together and bring the water to a boil. Remove the water mixture from the heat, add the filled tea ball, and let the tea steep for 5 to 8 minutes. Remove the tea ball.

Add the sugar and stir to dissolve. Cool the tea to room temperature. Strain the tea into a pitcher, stir in the milk, and then refrigerate the tea to chill it. Serve over ice.

PEACH LEMONADE

I make this refreshing lemonade when I have a supply of peaches from the farmers' market. It is sweet, tangy, peachy, and delicious.

SERVES 8

FOR THE LEMONADE

2 quarts water

¾ cup sugar

2 cups Peach Purée (recipe follows)

¾ cup fresh lemon juice (about 6 lemons)

FOR THE PEACH PURÉE

4 medium peaches

TO MAKE THE LEMONADE

In a medium saucepan over medium heat, combine the water and sugar. Stir until the sugar dissolves. Bring the mixture to a boil, reduce the heat, and let the mixture simmer for 2 minutes. Remove the simple syrup from the heat and let it cool to room temperature.

TO MAKE THE PEACH PURÉE

Lightly score an X on the bottom of each peach. Blanch the peaches in a large pot of boiling water for 60 seconds. Remove the peaches with a spoon and place them in a bowl of ice water for a few seconds. Peel and pit the peaches. Purée the peaches in a food processor or blender.

TO ASSEMBLE

Stir the peach purée into the saucepan with the simple syrup. Pour the purée mixture into a large pitcher, add the lemon juice, and stir to combine. Refrigerate the lemonade until it is well chilled.

FORBIDDEN FLAVORS

I WAS SIX YEARS old when Martin Luther King Jr. delivered his 1963 "I Have a Dream" speech. As I listened to his speech on the radio, his baritone voice commanded my attention. His words gave me hope for my future as a little Black girl living in a segregated society. Moved by Dr. King's speech, I decided to strive for equality by demonstrating. Our community in Chapel Hill, North Carolina, worked together and marched toward freedom.

It all began with the Black students of the segregated Lincoln High School, including my first cousin Albert Williams, on my mother's side. The 1960 Greensboro lunch counter sit-ins were an important influence, and inspired the students to organize their own demonstrations. They held meetings and planned sit-ins at Chapel Hill's segregated lunch counters, movie theaters, and restaurants. They are known as the Chapel Hill Nine.

I marched alongside family members, neighbors, and UNC students. From inside our home, which was adjacent to Franklin Street, I could hear the faint sound of the marchers' voices singing from a distance, like a church choir approaching the choir stand. The marchers started at Saint Joseph CME Church. The sound got louder as they came closer. Heading toward downtown, they would pick up other folks as they approached.

I always ran outside and waited in our front yard. As they passed our house, we joined in. The size of the crowd and the sound expanded. We sang, "What are you marching for? Freedom! What are you marching for? Freedom! What are you marching for? FREEDOM FREEDOM FREEDOM!" My hope expanded during those marches. I learned early on that I must be part of the change that was starting to happen all around me. We continued to march.

Adults and children protest for civil rights on Franklin Street.

It took years of tireless, hard-

The Chapel Hill Nine sit-in inspired supporters of all backgrounds to continue the protests at Colonial Drug.

fought, and peaceful protests—planning, picketing, sit-ins, and marches—from February 1960 until July 2, 1964, when President Lyndon B. Johnson signed the Civil Rights Act into law. Still, some places resisted desegregation, holding out until the mounting pressure from the protests left them no choice. Thanks to the bravery of the Chapel Hill Nine, whose actions united our community, the dream became a reality, but only with faith and time.

Now, it was time to enjoy the fruits of our labor, not simply for what was inside those stores but also as a community and a nation. We had stood up for what was right and prevailed. When I finally stepped inside those once-forbidden places, I felt excited, then a sense of belonging and accomplishment came over me as I took in the vast and varied sights, smells, and sounds. I earned great satisfaction there once I entered. I was only seven years old, but I knew this was history, and I was part of it.

I had faith that change would come, that one day I would be able to enter any business freely. But, until then, my mother cautioned my siblings and me to keep to ourselves and not respond when, while visiting downtown Franklin Street, white people addressed us unfavorably because of the color of our skin. The divide did not affect my self-esteem, nor did I feel detached from Chapel Hill. My confidence came from a host of Black community leaders, including shopkeepers who provided for our needs; church ministers, deacons, and Sunday school teachers who taught us that *Jesus loves all the little children*; social clubs like the Elks, that gave us hayrides, Easter egg hunts, and dance parties; and orga-

My mother as a member of the women's auxiliary of the Elks Lodge, Queen Esther Temple #696.

nizations like the Willing Workers that set the example and encouraged us to give to those in need; the schoolteachers who loved and encouraged us; the teenagers who taught us to swim, and were our lifeguards while we swam; and our neighbors who watched over us. Most of all, I drew strength from my mother and her siblings.

Nourishing Northside: Chapel Hill's women serving meals.

Within these nurturing environments, the distinct flavor of our food terroir shaped our experiences. But there were flavors on Franklin Street that were denied to me because of segregation. Two places near my home, Colonial Drug Store and Long Meadow Farm Dairy Store, stood as reminders of where I was not welcome. Yet, both introduced me to what I considered new—and sometimes forbidden—flavors.

When we circulated about town on Sundays, Mama always required that my sisters and I stay together to support each other. Living in a university town gave us access to different places on campus. We appreciated the arts at Ackland Art Museum; we took walks under a canopy of flowers at Coker Arboretum; we took in plays at Forest Theatre; and we took a break from our long walks to sip water from the Old Well. But our favorite place was Morehead Planetarium, with its adjacent sundial and flower garden. Inside, there was the auditorium where splashes of light bounced off our bodies as we looked up at the celestial ceiling, with planets spinning and stars twinkling, drawing us into its constellations. Afterward, we turned our attention to the University of North Carolina architectural model, displayed in a different room near the rotunda.

Each time we walked toward campus, we passed Colonial Drug Store. Its window sign read, VISIT OUR TOY DEPARTMENT, but its retro lunch counter and soda fountain were off limits to me. I was too young to enter the store, but my older siblings and cousins could go inside to pick up items from the pharmacy or order a beverage to go. Still, they were never allowed to sit at the counter and were served last.

One Sunday, while the store was closed, I stopped and took a peek at what was inside. It held my curiosity like a kitten chasing after a rolling ball of yarn. I placed both hands on the windowpane and reached above my head, aiming to keep my balance while I stood on the tips of my toes while I stretched my long legs. My forehead felt the cool touch of the glass as my face pressed against the glass display window. I was positioning my body to see what was on the vertical shelves toward the back of the dimly lit store. I also wanted to see the toy department and the rows of candy shelves near the front of the store. My imagination took over—I pictured myself climbing onto a round, cushioned stool at the lunch counter, ordering an ice cream soda, and spinning around as I pleased.

Each time I passed the drugstore after that, I wondered what new flavors awaited me—if only I were allowed to step inside.

Beginning at the age of seven, I was free to enter and shop in any business I wanted, giving me a sense of new adventures. And that meant, for the first time, stepping inside Colonial Drug Store to sit at the counter and place my own order for my favorite treat: the Big O—a deliciously sweet orangeade.

John Carswell, the owner, pharmacist, and soda jerk known as Big John, stood behind the counter. He was a tall man, from which he might have gotten his nickname, and had a slightly curved posture. He never smiled or made small talk, and only asked, "What can I get for you?" and stated the amount owed.

After taking in the display of home and garden and word puzzle magazines by the window, I always got my order to go—a casual stroll in my neighborhood while sipping my Big O was much more enjoyable than remaining inside.

I'm guessing Big John caught the retirement bug, or he closed due to Chapel Hill's changing and growing food scene. Big John's Colonial Drug Store closed in 1996 when I was 39 years old. It was the first place the Chapel Hill Nine staged their sit-in.

Northside Community Leaders

THE BIG O

At Colonial Drug Store in Chapel Hill, the Big O was a drink I looked forward to whenever I had saved enough money. Big John, the owner and soda jerk, made it with careful precision. He would slice each orange in half, place it against a hand-crank juicer, then pour the extracted liquid into a stainless steel shaker. He added a pump or two of syrup, stirred it into a tall cup, topped it with water, then served it over crushed ice.

Later, as an adult, I realized that Big John had a passion for his beverage craft. And ultimately, he was proud to create the best Big O he could, even for me, a little Black girl no longer living in a segregated society.

SERVES 6

FOR THE SIMPLE SYRUP

1 cup water

1 cup sugar

FOR THE ORANGEADE

2 cups freshly squeezed orange juice (about 8 large oranges)

¼ cup fresh lemon juice (about 2 lemons)

¼ cup Simple Syrup (from recipe above)

3 cups water

Crushed ice

TO MAKE THE SIMPLE SYRUP

In a small saucepan over medium heat, combine the water and sugar. Stir until the sugar dissolves. Bring to a boil. Let cool to room temperature. Store in the refrigerator for up to 4 weeks.

TO MAKE THE BIG O

Stir together the orange juice, lemon juice, ¼ cup simple syrup, and water in a large pitcher. Refrigerate the orangeade until chilled, about 2 hours. When ready to serve, fill the glasses with crushed ice and fill to the top with orangeade.

PEANUT RUM AND COKE

This rum cocktail reminds me of my grandfather Bill, who loved adding salted peanuts to bottles of ice-cold Coca-Cola—a tradition he, of course, passed down to my generation. I can picture him sitting on the back porch relaxing with his favorite snack. This refreshing drink blends sweet and salty flavors with a mouthful of crunch. Adding rum turns this nostalgic beverage into a cocktail. For a fun party starter, set out bottles of Coke in an ice-filled bucket, along with a bowl of peanuts, a small scoop, and a bottle of rum, so guests can mix their own.

SERVES 1

- 1 (6-ounce) bottle Coca-Cola, ice cold
- 1½ ounces light rum
- ¼ cup salted peanuts

First, drink enough Coke to empty the neck of the bottle. Add the rum and peanuts to the bottle, then use your finger to push the peanuts down past the neck of the bottle and into the soda. Be ready to catch the overflow of fizz with your mouth.

RECYCLE ME
SEE YOU AGAIN SOON!
Coca-Cola
ORIGINAL TASTE
Delicious & Refreshing

BIG DIPPER COCKTAIL

The Big Dipper, served in a tall hurricane glass, became a hit after Laura Edwards suggested to her Pi Beta Phi sorority sisters that they should support the new bar at Mama Dip's Kitchen. So much so that at the beginning of the fall semester, at the end of the school year, and when a member turned 21 (the legal drinking age in North Carolina), a large group would gather to celebrate with a toast.

We now serve the Big Dipper Cocktail at our family gatherings. For Christmas celebrations, we rent a beverage fountain and have Big Dippers flowing during our evening after-dinner party.

SERVES 6

1 cup Southern Comfort
½ cup brandy
½ cup orange liqueur
½ cup crème de almond
½ cup orange juice
½ cup pineapple juice
½ cup fresh lemon juice
½ cup fresh lime juice
Ice
Orange slices and cherries for garnish

Pour all the ingredients except the ice into a large pitcher and stir well.

For each drink, pour ¾ cup into an ice-filled cocktail shaker. Shake well to chill. Strain into a tall glass filled with ice. Garnish with an orange slice and a cherry.

CHAPEL HILL COCKTAIL

This drink, using the Old-Fashioned Lemonade recipe (page 214), was created by my cousin, Larry Williams, and is a cheer to Chapel Hill, North Carolina.

In 1978, it became legal for restaurants in North Carolina to sell liquor by the drink. Some years later, Mama added a bar to Mama Dip's Kitchen and sent my cousin, Larry Williams, to bartending school in Raleigh. He created the bar program and worked along with a family friend, Earl Hargraves, who was an experienced bartender. When I wasn't busy waiting tables, I would hang out at the bar to learn the art of bartending. From Larry, I learned how to make an accurate pour without using a cocktail jigger, and how to create a delicious cocktail. Earl taught me how to make multiple cocktails at one time, which came in handy.

SERVES 1

Ice cubes

2 ounces Old-Fashioned Lemonade (page 214)

1 ounce bourbon

½ ounce triple sec

Fill a cocktail shaker with ice. Add the remaining ingredients and shake well, about 10 seconds. Strain the drink into an ice-filled, old-fashioned glass, or for a special touch, place a single ice ball in the glass before pouring.

MENUS

SOUTHERN HOSPITALITY comes in all shapes and sizes. It ranges from inviting someone to share in a slice of freshly baked cake, gathering a few friends for a spontaneous get-together, a full-fledged dinner party, or a tea party to a holiday spread with family and friends. You can pretty much tell which holiday it is based on which dishes are served. I grew up during an era when there was a set time to eat, and the family would gather at the family table to enjoy the meal and each other's company, talking and having fun with each other. As the years have gone by, kids have gotten married and moved away. So when I start reminiscing about what Mama called "the good old days," I know it's time to have a party to bring family and friends together again.

Looking back, I realize many people and events influenced my love for sharing a gracious table with others, because they had taken the time to share them with me. This sort of hospitality is a learned habit. What a great feeling!

I'm just like my mom; I feel a child-like joy while in the kitchen, and receive pleasure surrounding myself with family and friends who need a break from the hustle and bustle of everyday life, creating moments when we can sit back, relax, and enjoy ourselves over good food and libations. My selection of menus includes both the traditional Southern dishes found during my family's holiday season as well as the more modern way that I entertain at my table.

SOUTHERN SNACK BOARD AND COCKTAILS

Fried Walnuts

Cheddar Cheese Relish

Sardine and Cream Cheese Spread

Ham-Stuffed Eggs

BLT Crackers

Fresh Okra Fritters

Chapel Hill Cocktail

Peanut Rum and Coke

BREAKFAST FOR DINNER

Shrimp and Salami Egg Scramble

Onion Potatoes

Pimento Cheese Biscuits

Apple Crisp with Cinnamon Whipped Cream

EAT TO GOOD LUCK, GOOD HEALTH, AND LOTS OF MONEY FOR THE NEW YEAR

Country-Style Pork Spare Ribs

Okra and Black-Eyed Peas Pilaf

Braised Collard Greens

Sweet Potato and Apple Bake

Coconut Cake with Coconut Sour Cream Frosting

EASTER SUNDAY DINNER

Corn Bread and Pickle-Crusted Bone-In Spiral Cut Ham

Fried Chicken

Stewed Corn

Asparagus and Sweet Pepper Salad

Buttermilk Yeast Rolls

Chocolate Cake with Caramel Pecan Fudge Frosting

JUNETEENTH CELEBRATION DINNER

BLT Crackers

Smothered Fried Chicken with Andouille Sausage

Mashed Potatoes and Turnips with Thyme Butter

Country-Fried Cabbage

Buttermilk Yeast Rolls

Beet, Apricot, and Goat Cheese Salad

Goat Cheese Pound Cake

Sweet Potato Custard Ice Cream

GAME NIGHT

Spiced Cocktail Peanuts

Pinto Bean Bowl with Fatback Corn Bread Crumble and Onion Jam

Shrimp Potato Salad

Caesar Salad with Arugula and Garlic Croutons

THANKSGIVING BUFFET

Fried Turkey with Giblet Gravy, Mortadella Corn Bread Dressing, and Cranberry Compote

Braised Beef Short Ribs

String Beans with Fresh Herbs

Braised Collard Greens

Macaroni and Cheese

Buttermilk Yeast Rolls

Yellow Layer Cake with Pumpkin Frosting

Lemon Chess Pie with Cardamom

LET'S BRUNCH

Grits Casserole with Shrimp Gravy

Asparagus, Bacon, and Parmesan Omelet Pie

Strawberry, Romaine, and Red Onion Salad

Sweet Potato Corn Bread

AFTERWORD

INSPIRED BY MAMA'S tireless dedication and the joy she found in her work, I knew that keeping her dream alive and preserving her legacy meant embracing every aspect of the business she had built with love, and doing whatever it took to keep it going. I have bussed tables, waited tables, washed dishes, and mopped floors. I have baked cakes and pies, short-order cooked, cooked, managed a waitstaff and kitchen, and kept the books. I was my mother's assistant, traveling with her on her cookbook tours and assisting production crews on programs like *Good Morning America* and channels like QVC. I watched cooking shows and read food magazines, and my knowledge of cooking techniques and ingredients for cooking in my kitchen grew along the way. Still, Mama's kitchen formed my culinary foundation and provided me with the skills I've used for more than 50 years working in our family restaurant business and as a personal chef, caterer, and recipe developer.

Yet, despite my deep roots in the culinary world, I also nurtured dreams beyond my mother's kitchen. I imagined a career in fashion and design, once dreaming of becoming a fashion buyer, and my friends suggested that I become a model—an idea that Mama strongly disagreed with. Needing an outlet for my creativity, I took on the responsibility of baking pies for the restaurant. I treated each crust like I was fluffing up a ruffle on a dress, and I sought perfection when crimping the dough along the edges of the pan.

When I started short-order cooking, long before I knew what a food stylist's role was in the kitchen, I wanted my plates of meat-and-two to be flawless, with the crispy, golden-fried catfish and a quarter of a fried chicken laying perfectly on the plate. That was where I could be creative, as Mama had already perfected the recipes for her kitchen.

Before I went to Mama for advice during my culinary growth, I cooked French, Italian, and Mexican dishes. I strictly followed recipes, taking precise measurements but found no gratification in the flavor or texture of my results. Although Mama encouraged me to explore new flavors, she said I first needed to master cooking recipes from my own heritage before I could successfully incorporate ingredients and techniques from other cultures. Mama told me that my roots were where I would learn the aroma, tastes, sights, sounds, and mouthfeel of traditional Southern cuisine, and that I needed to rely on these "sense" memories when experimenting with my new culinary efforts. My efforts to duplicate other cooking styles failed because I needed to know the tastes, smells, textures, sounds, and sights of the dishes I was attempting to replicate. After many failed experiments, I became aware of the connection between my food memories and roots, and I learned why Mama was right.

Four of my mother's elder siblings—Aunt Marie, Uncle Jim, Uncle Wilson, and Aunt Bernice—were particularly important to me while developing my sense of terroir. Aunt Marie showed me how the sustenance provided by animals of the backwoods were part of the region's foodways. Uncle Jim taught me about raising livestock and poultry. Uncle Wilson introduced me to the pleasures of gardening through the seasons. And Aunt Bernice, a pivotal and unsung figure in Chapel Hill food history, not only taught my mother how to cook traditional Southern food, but also, as a cook at a local Greek restaurant, helped usher in the town's taste for international flavors and expanded my young palate. Today, I have plenty of global dishes to choose from: African, Indian, Turkish, Thai, Japanese, Korean, Persian, and Malaysian. All offer flavors that pair well with Southern ingredients.

Expanding beyond my neighborhood mentors and Mama's kitchens, I now enjoy creating layers of flavors in my meals and making use of ever-changing ingredients, tools, and resources that Mama did not have access to when cooking on the farm and later for her family. Preserving and evolving is how I see Southern fusion cooking still taking place, due to the availability of a melting pot of ingredients and a growing blending of global cultures.

Just as Southern cooking continues to evolve, so too does the landscape of my childhood. On my summer and fall visits to my old neighborhood, I take a slow stroll to feel the pleasure of memories—memories of the families with whom I once had a weekly, or sometimes daily, connection. I stand and look at the house that I once lived in, and sense the place in the kitchen and the activities that I experienced. I appreciate the homes that my neighbors once lived in, recollecting the flavor clouds that came from each one as I walked past them on my way home for dinner from Hargraves Community Center.

The changes to the neighborhood that my mother foresaw decades ago have come to pass. Today, like many African American neighborhoods around the country, Northside is threatened by gentrification and the displacement of longtime residents. Northside joins communities in Savannah, Richmond, Houston, and elsewhere that are located in prime areas that attract higher-income residents and investors while replacing lower-income residents. The result is that the historical foundations of these neighborhoods are changing.

Most of the houses in Northside are still there, and the streets are still there, but most of the families have moved on and the homes are now desirable rentals for UNC students, mostly owned by landlords who live elsewhere.

I notice the sparse silence of a place that was once occupied by hundreds of children on its playground, playing games like horseshoes and shuffleboard, and swimming in the pool. Inside Hargraves Community Center, I can imagine kids playing bumper pool, ping-pong, billiards, and board games, as my brothers and sisters and I once did, and dancing to the latest tunes performed live by Kenny Mann and the Liquid Pleasure Band, a group of teenagers from the Northside community.

I will never forget attending my first day care in the basement of Hargraves Community Center, and how I learned to dislike spinach because the cook there turned it to a pulp. But I enjoy eating spinach now, cooking it with a little garlic and olive oil, just until it is wilted.

Whenever I walk past the house that once belonged to Mrs. Barbara Bynum—who was tall like my mother, and her daughters were tall like me—I remember how she looked out for us, even though we did not like her approach. I'm guessing Mrs. Bynum sat in her living room most of the time, because she would always come to her screen door as we walked by to let us know that we were laughing or talking too loudly, and she would tell our mothers so. We learned to respect her space and, after a little distance, we proceeded with our joyful time. Mrs. Bynum and her family no longer live there, and where their home once stood is now an empty lot. At the heart of the Northside community was how each family unit clung together and supported each other and their neighbors. That sense of community is changing, too.

And there are other changes. There are no more pecan trees, and my memorable plum tree no longer stands. The creek and bridge are gone and have been replaced by a road. No grape arbors remain, but some of the wild persimmon trees have survived.

Despite the incoming changes, there is hope for the Northside community, thanks especially to the work of the Marian Cheek Jackson Center for Saving and Making History. This nonprofit organization petitioned for the creation of the Northside Neighborhood Conservation District, special zoning established in 2004 aimed at preserving the look of our community. The Marian Cheek Jackson Center also records oral histories, preserving the memories of the natives who once lived there and the small group who still lives there—collecting historical information from Chapel Hill's African American locals so that we are known outside our community, and so our voices can be heard by future generations.

But nothing makes me prouder than expressing my sentiments as I tell the story of Mildred Edna Cotton Council—my mother, teacher, motivator, and mentor. Her strength, resilience, and passion for life continue to touch so many. From a young age, she understood the power of giving, beginning with a single pumpkin seed that she planted. She nurtured it, grew it, and shared its yield with others—even the birds.

I learned so much from my mother—not only through the meals she cooked but from the many roles she held in her lifetime. She was a hairstylist, maid, cook, restaurateur, author, and activist, but above all, she was a mother unlike any other. She may have had little at times, but she protected her children from knowing their state of poverty. She knew that progressive change was happening, and sticking to her heritage brought her great success and brought her back to the Northside.

The pumpkin seed that Mama planted took root in me, sprouting and giving life in many forms. Today, a new generation of Council women continues her legacy. Inspired by our mother's lessons on growth, learning, and sharing, my sister Annette "Neecy" Council launched Sweet Neecy Cake Mix Company in 2009—a line of all-natural Southern cake mixes. My niece, Erika Council, carries on the tradition in her own way as owner of Bomb Biscuit Company in Atlanta, serving up her signature biscuits to the community and sharing her expertise through her cookbook, *Still We Rise*.

My daughter, Tonya Council, who grew up in Mama Dip's Kitchen, is also a baker, chef, and entrepreneur. Her Pecan Crisp Cookies earned a spot on Oprah's influential list of "Favorite Things" in 2022, followed by her Cream Cheese Pound Cake in 2024—both inspired by my mother's signature flavors. Through her retail store, Sweet Tea & Cornbread: Shop South, Tonya connects with fellow entrepreneurs she meets along her food journey, offering a space to share and celebrate Southern artisan products.

My goal is to share the yield from that sprouted seed, continuing my mother's legacy of giving back to the community, no matter how much or how little we may have—and the importance of nurturing through food. I carry her dreams with me, just as I lived within Mama's story and found my own.

Southern cooking continues to evolve, but these recipes are my way of holding on to my foundation. I hope reading my stories brings back your own joyful memories, and that cooking these recipes tickles your taste buds and inspires you to give the gift of yourself through food and a well-set table—even if the dishes don't match. And, just as important, always invite children into your kitchen.

ACKNOWLEDGMENTS

WRITING *SOUTHERN ROOTS* has been a journey of love, memory, and flavor, brought to life by the incredible support, guidance, and inspiration from so many wonderful people.

I am deeply grateful to **Marcie Cohen Ferris**, dear friend and trusted mentor. Her insightful suggestion to make this a culinary memoir was pivotal, reshaping the book and leading to its publication. Marcie, your wisdom, vision, and beautiful foreword are invaluable gifts.

My heartfelt gratitude to **Regina Mahalek**, longtime champion of our family's culinary heritage. You were there for Mama's cookbooks, and you've been with me every step of the way with *Southern Roots*—from the initial proposal through the final proofs. You've been a steadfast friend, unwavering encourager, and trusted editorial guide.

To my agent, **Sharon Bowers**, thank you for taking on *Southern Roots* at the proposal stage, believing in its potential, and securing its perfect home with Countryman Press. Your support and advocacy gave me courage.

To my editor, **Ann Treistman**, thank you for your insightful vision in guiding *Southern Roots* to its final form as a traditional cookbook. Your patient expertise in shaping stories and recipes was invaluable. Special thanks to assistant editor **Maya Goldfarb**, for her instrumental role in the book's conceptual evolution. Thanks also to the entire **Countryman Press** team. Your dedication and enthusiasm were essential in bringing *Southern Roots* to readers.

My heartfelt thanks go to my photographer, **Anna Routh Barzin**, and food stylist, **Kelly Green**. Anna, thank you for your wonderful patience, energy, and passion throughout the entire process. Kelly, thank you for sharing your incredible talents and creative eye. My deep appreciation to the friends who helped bring this book to life: **Joselyn Williams** and **Regina Merritt**, for their energy and joy during photo shoots; **Jackie Beatty Smith**, for invaluable recipe testing and feedback; and **Sharon Davis** and **Nancie McDermott**, who did it all—testing recipes and prepping food for shoots. Your essential contributions are deeply appreciated.

To my family: Sharing my culinary journey with you has been a deep joy. While writing these stories, I truly felt your presence beside me.

To my amazing daughter, **Tonya Council**. It is one of the greatest joys of my life to watch you carry on Mama Dip's legacy with grace, strength, and passion. Through your wonderful businesses—Tonya's Cookies, Tonya's Café, and Sweet Tea & Cornbread—you honor our family's story daily. This book celebrates the deep roots we share, roots you tend so beautifully. I am endlessly proud of the remarkable woman and business owner you have become. I love you.

To the inspiring Chapel Hill community—the farmers, home cooks, storytellers, and the Marian Cheek Jackson Center who uphold our culinary heritage with such dedication. Your collective passion is woven into the fabric of *Southern Roots,* enriching every page.

And finally, to you, the reader. Thank you for welcoming *Southern Roots* into your home. It's my hope that these recipes and stories bring warmth to your kitchen and joy to your heart, reflecting the love that inspired them.

INDEX

Boldface indicates an illustration.

anchovy fillets in Caesar Salad with Arugula and Garlic Croutons, **82,** 83
Andalouse Sauce, Fried Chicken Lollipops with, 50, **51–53**
Andouille Sausage, Smothered Fried Chicken with, 116–117
apples
  Apple Coleslaw, **98,** 99
  Apple Crisp with Cinnamon Whipped Cream, 181
  Sweet Potato and Apple Bake, 107
apricots
  Beet, Apricot, and Goat Cheese Salad, **76,** 77
  Cranberry Compote, 163, **165**
artichokes in Spinach, Parmesan, and Artichoke Gratin, **104,** 105
arugula
  Caesar Salad with Arugula and Garlic Croutons, **82,** 83
  Arugula and Egg Salad Tea Sandwiches, 169, **171**
  Watermelon Salad, 78
asparagus
  Asparagus, Bacon, and Parmesan Omelet Pie, 42, **43**
  Asparagus and Sweet Pepper Salad, 86
  Cream of Asparagus Soup with Mushroom Ragù, 70–71, **71**

bacon
  Asparagus, Bacon, and Parmesan Omelet Pie, 42, **43**
  BLT Crackers, **60,** 61
  Cheddar Cheese Relish, 58, **59**
  Chocolate Bread Pudding with Candied Bacon, 198, **199**
  Grits Casserole with Shrimp Gravy, **30,** 31
bananas
  Banana and Chocolate Coffee Cake with Rum Glaze, 41
  Banana Pudding with Chocolate Meringue, 180
beans
  Pinto Bean Bowl with Fatback Corn Bread Crumble and Onion Jam, 124–125, **125**
  String Beans with Fresh Herbs, 102, **103**
beef. *See also* ground beef
  Braised Beef Short Ribs, **128,** 129
  Prime Rib Roast with Yorkshire Pudding, 156
beef broth in Braised Beef Short Ribs, **128,** 129
Beet, Apricot, and Goat Cheese Salad, **76,** 77
beverages. *See* Drinks
Big Dipper Cocktail, **226**, 227
"Big John." *See* Carswell, John
The Big O, **222,** 223
Bill's Bar-B-Q, 15–18, 22, 44, 100
Biscuits, Pimento Cheese, 28, **29**
Black-Eyed Peas Pilaf, Okra and, 150, **151**
BLT Crackers, **60,** 61
Bomb Biscuit Company, 23, 238
bourbon in Chapel Hill Cocktail, **228**, 229
Braised Beef Short Ribs, **128,** 129
Braised Collard Greens, 90, **91**
brandy in Big Dipper Cocktail, **226**, 227
bread and butter pickles. *See also* relish
  Corn Bread and Pickle-Crusted Bone-In Spiral Cut Ham, 154, **155**
Bread and Butter Pudding, Swiss Chard and Chick-pea, 153
bread crumbs
  Asparagus, Bacon, and Parmesan Omelet Pie, 42, **43**
  Chicken Croquettes with Butter and Herb Cream Sauce, 118, **119,** 120
  Chocolate Bread Pudding with Candied Bacon, 198, **199**
  Spinach, Parmesan, and Artichoke Gratin, **104,** 105
Bread Pudding, Chocolate, with Candied Bacon, 198, **199**
breads. *See also* biscuits; corn bread; crusty bread
  Buttermilk Yeast Rolls, 157
  Gorgonzola and Walnut Scones, **172,** 173

breads (*continued*)
Sweet Bread with Raspberries, 189
Sweet Potato Hot Cross Buns, 147
Breakfast and Brunch, 25–47
Asparagus, Bacon, and Parmesan Omelet Pie, 42, **43**
Banana and Chocolate Coffee Cake with Rum Glaze, 41
Cheese Grits with Corn Kernels, 32
Country Ham with Milk Gravy, 35
Grated Sweet Potato Pancakes, 38, **39**
Grits Casserole with Shrimp Gravy, **30,** 31
Monte Cristo Sandwich, **36,** 37
Pimento Cheese Biscuits, 28, **29**
Plum and Nectarine Yogurt Bowl with Wildflower Honey Granola, 47
Shrimp and Salami Egg Scramble, 33
Zucchini and Tomato Frittata, 34
Brûléed Corn Pudding, 108
brunch. *See* Breakfast and Brunch
buttermilk
Buttermilk Yeast Rolls, 157
Chocolate Cake with Caramel Pecan Fudge Frosting, 196–197
Pinto Bean Bowl with Fatback Corn Bread Crumble and Onion Jam, 124–125, **125**
Sweet Potato Corn Bread, 54

cabbage
Apple Coleslaw, **98,** 99
Carolina Burger, 122–123, **123**
Country-Fried Cabbage, 95
Shrimp Croquettes with Remoulade Coleslaw on a Bun, 137, **138,** 139
Caesar Salad with Arugula and Garlic Croutons, **82,** 83
cakes
Banana and Chocolate Coffee Cake with Rum Glaze, 41
Chocolate Cake with Caramel Pecan Fudge Frosting, 196–197
Coconut Cake with Coconut Sour Cream Frosting, 177
Fresh Fruit Pineapple Upside-Down Cake, 192
Goat Cheese Pound Cake, 184, **185**
homemade, 176
Strawberry Biscuit Cake, **182**, 183
Yellow Layer Cake with Pumpkin Frosting, 178–179, **179**
Cantaloupe and Raspberry Milkshake, 208
Caramel Pecan Fudge Frosting, 196–197
Cardamom Iced Tea, 215
Carolina Burger, 122–123, **123**
Carswell, John "Big John," 221, 223
casseroles
Eggplant and Tomato Casserole, 126
Grits Casserole with Shrimp Gravy, **30,** 31
Chapel Hill (North Carolina), 15, 19–20, 22–23, 100–101, 218–221
Chapel Hill Cocktail, **228**, 229
Chapel Hill Nine, 22, 218–221
cheddar cheese
Carolina Burger, 122–123, **123**
Cheddar Cheese Relish, 58, **59**
Grits Casserole with Shrimp Gravy, **30,** 31
Macaroni and Cheese, 96, **97**
Pimento Cheese Biscuits, 28, **29**
cheese. *See also* cheddar cheese; cream cheese; feta cheese; goat cheese; Parmesan cheese; provolone cheese; ricotta cheese; Swiss cheese
Cheese Grits with Corn Kernels, 32
cherries in Fresh Fruit Pineapple Upside-Down Cake, 192
chicken
Chicken and Drop Dumplings, 114, **115**
Chicken Croquettes with Butter and Herb Cream Sauce, 118, **119,** 120
Fried Chicken Lollipops with Andalouse Sauce, 50, **51–53**
Smothered Fried Chicken with Andouille Sausage, 116–117
chicken broth
Cream of Asparagus Soup with Mushroom Ragù, 70–71, **71**
Cream of Turnip Soup with Crispy Greens, 75
chickpeas in Swiss Chard and Chickpea Bread and Butter Pudding, 153
chilies. *See* jalapeño peppers; piquillo peppers
Chilled Cucumber Soup with Smoked Salmon, 74
Chocolate Bread Pudding with Candied Bacon, 198, **199**
Chocolate Cake with Caramel Pecan Fudge Frosting, 196–197
chocolate chips
Banana and Chocolate Coffee Cake with Rum Glaze, 41
Chocolate Bread Pudding with Candied Bacon, 198, **199**
Oatmeal Peanut Butter Bars, 193
Sweet Potato and Pecan Pie, **190,** 191
Chocolate Meringue, Banana Pudding with, 180
Cinnamon Whipped Cream, Apple Crisp with, 181
Claiborne, Craig, 11–12, 20, 22
Coconut Cake with Coconut Sour Cream Frosting, 177

coconut milk
Coconut Cake with Coconut Sour Cream Frosting, 177
Grated Sweet Potato Pancakes, 38, **39**
Coffee Cake, Banana and Chocolate, with Rum Glaze, 41
Coke, Peanut Rum and, 224, **225**
Coleslaw, Apple, **98,** 99
collard greens
Braised Collard Greens, 90, **91**
Collard Greens and Italian Sausage Lasagna, 130, **131,** 132
Colonial Drug Store, 22, **219**, 220–221, 223
"Come Sunday" tradition, 127
cookbooks, historical and regional, 72–73
cookies. *See* Oatmeal Peanut Butter Bars
corn
Brûléed Corn Pudding, 108
Cheese Grits with Corn Kernels, 32
Mama's Grilled Corn on the Cob, 146
Purple Hull Peas and Corn, 101
Stewed Corn, **92,** 93
corn bread
Corn Bread and Pickle-Crusted Bone-In Spiral Cut Ham, 154, **155**
Mortadella Corn Bread Dressing, 163, **164**
Sweet Potato Corn Bread, 54
cornmeal
Fresh Okra Fritters, **66,** 67
Fried Green Tomato Parmesan, 121
Lemon Chess Pie with Cardamom, 200
Pinto Bean Bowl with Fatback Corn Bread Crumble and Onion Jam, 124–125, **125**
Shrimp Croquettes with Remoulade Coleslaw on a Bun, 137, **138,** 139
Sweet Potato Corn Bread, 54
Cotton, Ed (mother of Mama Dip), 13
Cotton, Effie (mother of Mama Dip), 13
Cotton, Jim (brother of Mama Dip), 130, **130**, 236
Cotton, Wilson (brother of Mama Dip), 57, **57**, 236
Council, Anita Spring, 11–12, 13–14, 22
Council, Annette "Neecy" (sister of Spring), 13, 23, 167, 238
Council, Erika (niece of Spring), 23, 238
Council, Geary (brother of Spring), 13
Council, Joe (father of Spring), 13, 40
Council, Joe, Jr. (brother of Spring), 13
Council, Julia (sister of Spring), 13
Council, Mildred Edna "Mama Dip" (née Cotton), 6, 12, 13, 22, 26–27, **219**
Council, Norma (sister of Spring), 13, 94
Council, Sandra "Lane" (sister of Spring), 13, 17, 45, 167
Council, Tonya (daughter of Spring), 12, 23
Council, William (brother of Spring), 13
Country-Fried Cabbage, 95
Country Ham with Milk Gravy, 35
Country-Style Pork Spare Ribs, 133
Crab Dip, Hot, 63
crackers. *See also* Ritz crackers
BLT Crackers, **60,** 61
Ham Terrine with Ritz Crackers, 62
Hot Crab Dip, 63
Sardine and Cream Cheese Spread, 64, **65**
Shrimp Croquettes with Remoulade Coleslaw on a Bun, 137, **138,** 139
Cranberry Compote, 163, **165**
cream cheese
Cucumber and Jalapeño Tea Sandwiches, 168, **171**
Grape and Walnut Salad, 79
Hot Crab Dip, 63
Pimento Cheese Biscuits, 28, **29**
Sardine and Cream Cheese Spread, 64, **65**
Shrimp and Salami Egg Scramble, 33
Yellow Layer Cake with Pumpkin Frosting, 178–179, **79**
Cream of Asparagus Soup with Mushroom Ragù, 70–71, **71**
Cream of Turnip Soup with Crispy Greens, 75
crème de almond in Big Dipper Cocktail, **226**, 227
croquettes
Chicken Croquettes with Butter and Herb Cream Sauce, 118, **119,** 120
Shrimp Croquettes with Remoulade Coleslaw on a Bun, 137, **138,** 139
crusty bread in Monte Cristo Sandwich, **36,** 37
cucumbers
Chilled Cucumber Soup with Smoked Salmon, 74
Iceberg Wedges with Cucumbers and Black Forest Ham, 80, **81**
Cucumber and Jalapeño Tea Sandwiches, 168, **171**

Danziger, Edward G., 194
Danziger's Old World Candy Shop, 194–195
A Date with a Dish (De Knight), 72–73
Desserts, 175–211. *See also* ice cream
Apple Crisp with Cinnamon Whipped Cream, 181
Banana Pudding with Chocolate Meringue, 180
Cantaloupe and Raspberry Milkshake, 208
Chocolate Bread Pudding with Candied Bacon, 198, **199**
Chocolate Cake with Caramel Pecan Fudge Frosting, 196–197
Coconut Cake with Coconut Sour Cream Frosting, 177
Fresh Fruit Pineapple Upside-Down Cake, 192

Desserts (*continued*)
Goat Cheese Pound Cake, 184, **185**
Lemon Chess Pie with Cardamom, 200
Oatmeal Peanut Butter Bars, 193
Orange Cream Punch, **210**, 211, **211**
Strawberry Biscuit Cake, **182**, 183
Sweet Bread with Raspberries, 189
Sweet Potato and Pecan Pie, **190,** 191
Yellow Layer Cake with Pumpkin Frosting, 178–179, **179**
dining table, importance in the home, 89
Dip's Country Kitchen, 11, 18–21, 22–23
Drinks, 212–229
Big Dipper Cocktail, **226**, 227
The Big O, **222,** 223
Cardamom Iced Tea, 214
Chapel Hill Cocktail, **228**, 229
Old-Fashioned Lemonade, 214
Orange Cream Punch, **210,** 211, **211**
Peach Lemonade, 216, **217**
Peanut Rum and Coke, 224, **225**
dump cooking, 27
dumplings, 111–113
Chicken and Drop Dumplings, 114, **115**

Eggplant and Tomato Casserole, 126
eggs
Arugula and Egg Salad Tea Sandwiches, 169, **171**
Asparagus, Bacon, and Parmesan Omelet Pie, 42, **43**
Banana and Chocolate Coffee Cake with Rum Glaze, 41
Brûléed Corn Pudding, 108
Fried Green Tomato Parmesan, 121
Grated Sweet Potato Pancakes, 38, **39**
Grits Casserole with Shrimp Gravy, **30**, 31
Ham-Stuffed Eggs, 68
Monte Cristo Sandwich, **36,** 37
Shrimp and Salami Egg Scramble, 33
Sweet Potato Corn Bread, 54
Tangy Potato Salad, 94
Zucchini and Tomato Frittata, 34

fatback, 90
Braised Collard Greens, 90, **91**
Country-Fried Cabbage, 95
Pinto Bean Bowl with Corn Bread Crumble and Onion Jam, 124–125, **125**
Stewed Corn, **92,** 93
feta cheese
Watermelon Salad, 78
Zucchini and Tomato Frittata, 34
fish. *See* salmon; seafood; shrimp
foraging, 44–46
Fresh Fruit Pineapple Upside-Down Cake, 192
Fresh Okra Fritters, **66,** 67
Fried Chicken Lollipops with Andalouse Sauce, 50, **51–53**
Fried Green Tomato Parmesan, 121
Fried Turkey with Giblet Gravy, Mortadella Corn Bread Dressing, and Cranberry Compote, **160,** 161–163, **164**, **165**
Fried Walnuts, 144, **145**
Frittata, Zucchini and Tomato, 34
Fritters, Fresh Okra, **66,** 67
frostings
Caramel Pecan Fudge Frosting, 196–197
Coconut Sour Cream Frosting, 177
Pumpkin Frosting, 178–179, **179**
Rum Glaze, 41

Giblet Gravy, 161
Ginger Snap Ice Cream, **206**, 207
goat cheese
Beet, Apricot, and Goat Cheese Salad, **76,** 77
Goat Cheese Pound Cake, 184, **185**
Gorgonzola and Walnut Scones, **172,** 173
Granola, Plum and Nectarine Yogurt Bowl with Wildflower Honey, 47
Grape and Walnut Salad, 79
grape tomatoes
Iceberg Wedges with Cucumbers and Black Forest Ham, 80, **81**
Watermelon Salad, 78
Zucchini and Tomato Frittata, 34
Grated Sweet Potato Pancakes, 38, **39**
green tomatoes in Fried Green Tomato Parmesan, 121
grits
Cheese Grits with Corn Kernels, 32
Grits Casserole with Shrimp Gravy, **30,** 31
ground beef. *See also* beef
Carolina Burger, 122–123, **123**

ham
Corn Bread and Pickle-Crusted Bone-In Spiral Cut Ham, 154, **155**
Country Ham with Milk Gravy, 35
Ham-Stuffed Eggs, 68
Ham Terrine with Ritz Crackers, 62
Iceberg Wedges with Cucumbers and Black Forest Ham, 80, **81**
Monte Cristo Sandwich, **36,** 37
Okra and Black-Eyed Peas Pilaf, 150, **151**
Pinto Bean Bowl with Fatback Corn Bread Crumble and Onion Jam, 124–125, **125**
Purple Hull Peas and Corn, 101

Hargraves Community Center, 16, 22, 166–167, 236–237
Holidays at Home, 141–174
Arugula and Egg Salad Tea Sandwiches, 169, **171**
Buttermilk Yeast Rolls, 157
Corn Bread and Pickle-Crusted Bone-In Spiral Cut Ham, 154, **155**
Cranberry Compote, 163, **165**
Cucumber and Jalapeño Tea Sandwiches, 168, **171**
Fried Turkey with Giblet Gravy, Mortadella Corn Bread Dressing, and Cranberry Compote, **160,** 161–163, **164, 165**
Fried Walnuts, 144, **145**
Gorgonzola and Walnut Scones, **172,** 173
Lemon Curd, 174, **174**
Mama's Grilled Corn on the Cob, 146
Mortadella Corn Bread Dressing, 163, **164**
Okra and Black-Eyed Peas Pilaf, 150, **151**
Prime Rib Roast with Yorkshire Pudding, 156
Mashed Potatoes and Turnips with Thyme Butter, **148,** 149
Sweet Potato Hot Cross Buns, 147
Swiss Chard and Chickpea Bread and Butter Pudding, 153
Tomato and Shrimp Butter Tea Sandwiches, 170, **171**
homemade cakes, 176
Hot Crab Dip, 63

iceberg lettuce
BLT Crackers, **60,** 61
Iceberg Wedges with Cucumbers and Black Forest Ham, 80, **81**
ice cream, 201, **202,** 203
Cantaloupe and Raspberry Milkshake, 208
Ginger Snap Ice Cream, **206,** 207
Orange Cream Punch, **210,** 211, **211**
Peach and Citrus Ice Cream, 209
Sweet Potato Custard Ice Cream, **202,** 204, **205**
Iced Tea, Cardamom, 215
Italian Sausage, Collards and, Lasagna, 130, **131,** 132

jalapeño peppers
Braised Collard Greens, 90, **91**
Country-Style Pork Spare Ribs, 133
Cucumber and Jalapeño Tea Sandwiches, 168, **171**

King, Martin Luther, Jr., 16, 22, 218
Kool-Aid in a teacup, 166–167

Lamb Chops, Pan-Fried, 134
Lasagna, Collards and Italian Sausage, 130, **131,** 132
Lemon Chess Pie with Cardamom, 200
Lemon Curd, 174, **174**
lemon juice
Big Dipper Cocktail, **226,** 227
The Big O, **222,** 223
Lemon Chess Pie with Cardamom, 200
Lemon Curd, 174, **174**
Old-Fashioned Lemonade, 214
Peach Lemonade, 216, **217**
lettuce. *See* iceberg lettuce; romaine lettuce
lima beans, 89
lime juice in Big Dipper Cocktail, **226,** 227
liquors. *See* rum
Long Meadow Farm Dairy Store, 201–203, **201,** 220

Macaroni and Cheese, 96, **97**
Mae, Mrs. Charlie, 17, 44
Mains, 109–139
Braised Beef Short Ribs, **128,** 129
Carolina Burger, 122–123, **123**
Chicken and Drop Dumplings, 114, **115**
Chicken Croquettes with Butter and Herb Cream Sauce, 118, **119,** 120
Collards and Italian Sausage Lasagna, 130, **131,** 132
Country-Style Pork Spare Ribs, 133
Eggplant and Tomato Casserole, 126
Fried Green Tomato Parmesan, 121
Pan-Fried Lamb Chops, 134
Pecan and Herb-Crusted Salmon, 135
Pinto Bean Bowl with Fatback Corn Bread Crumble and Onion Jam, 124–125, **125**
Shrimp Croquettes with Remoulade Coleslaw on a Bun, 137, **138,** 139
Shrimp Potato Salad, 136
Smothered Fried Chicken with Andouille Sausage, 116–117
Mama Dip's Family Cookbook, 13, 23
Mama Dip's Kitchen (cookbook), 13, 23, 108
Mama Dip's Kitchen (restaurant), 13, 21, 23, 89, 101, 108, 112, 152, 238
Mama's Grilled Corn on the Cob, 146
Marian Cheek Jackson Center for Saving and Making History, 23, 240
Mashed Potatoes and Turnips with Thyme Butter, **148,** 149
Mason, Annie Mae, 184, 186–187
McClelland, Annie Pearl, 187–188
menus, 231–233
Meringue, Chocolate, Banana Pudding with, 180
Milkshake, Cantaloupe and Raspberry, 208
Minor, Bill (paternal grandfather of Spring), 15, 22
Minor, Mary (paternal grandmother of Spring), 22
Monte Cristo Sandwich, **36,** 37
Mortadella Corn Bread Dressing, 163, **164**

mozzarella cheese
Collards and Italian Sausage Lasagna, 130, **131,** 132
Fried Green Tomato Parmesan, 121
mushrooms
Chicken Croquettes with Butter and Herb Cream Sauce, 118, **119,** 120
Cream of Asparagus Soup with Mushroom Ragù, 70–71, **71**

NC Made, 23
nectarines in Plum and Nectarine Yogurt Bowl with Wildflower Honey Granola, 47
Northside (Chapel Hill), 11, 15, 20, 44–46, 220–221, 236–238
nuts. *See* peanuts; pecans; walnuts

Oatmeal Peanut Butter Bars, 193
oats
Apple Crisp with Cinnamon Whipped Cream, 181
Oatmeal Peanut Butter Bars, 193
Plum and Nectarine Yogurt Bowl with Wildflower Honey Granola, 47
okra
Fresh Okra Fritters, **66,** 67
Okra and Black-Eyed Peas Pilaf, 150, **151**
Old-Fashioned Lemonade, 214
Chapel Hill Cocktail, **228,** 229
Omelet Pie, Asparagus, Bacon, and Parmesan, 42, **43**
onions. *See also* pearl onions; red onions
Braised Collard Greens, 90, **91**
Carolina Burger, 122–123, **123**
Chicken Croquettes with Butter and Herb Cream Sauce, 118, **119,** 120
Collards and Italian Sausage Lasagna, 130, **131,** 132
Country-Style Pork Spare Ribs, 133
Cucumber and Jalapeño Tea Sandwiches, 168, **171**
Giblet Gravy, 161
Mortadella Corn Bread Dressing, 163
Onion Jam, 125
Onion Potatoes, 106
Pinto Bean Bowl with Fatback Corn Bread Crumble and Onion Jam, 124–125, **125**
Shrimp Gravy, **30,** 31
Swiss Chard and Chickpea Bread and Butter Pudding, 153
Orange Cream Punch, **210,** 211, **211**
orange juice
Big Dipper Cocktail, **226,** 227
The Big O, **222,** 223
orange liqueur in Big Dipper Cocktail, **226,** 227

Pancakes, Grated Sweet Potato, 38, **39**
Pan-Fried Lamb Chops, 134
Parmesan cheese
Asparagus, Bacon, and Parmesan Omelet Pie, 42, **43**
Caesar Salad with Arugula and Garlic Croutons, **82,** 83
Cheese Grits with Corn Kernels, 32
Collards and Italian Sausage Lasagna, 130, **131,** 132
Fried Green Tomato Parmesan, 121
Macaroni and Cheese, 96, **97**
Mama's Grilled Corn on the Cob, 146
Mortadella Corn Bread Dressing, 163, **164**
Pan-Fried Lamb Chops, 134
Spinach, Parmesan, and Artichoke Gratin, **104,** 105
peach
Peach and Citrus Ice Cream, 209
Peach Lemonade, 216, **217**
peanut butter in Oatmeal Peanut Butter Bars, 193
Peanut Rum and Coke, 224, **225**
peanuts
Peanut Rum and Coke, 224, **225**
Spiced Cocktail Peanuts, **56,** 57
pearl onions in Braised Beef Short Ribs, **128,** 129
Peas, Purple Hull, and Corn, 101
pecans
Cheddar Cheese Relish, 58, **59**
Chocolate Cake with Caramel Pecan Fudge Frosting, 196–197
Pecan and Herb-Crusted Salmon, 135
Sweet Potato and Pecan Pie, **190,** 191
peppers. *See* jalapeño peppers; piquillo peppers
pickles. *See* bread and butter pickles; relish
pies, savory and sweet
Asparagus Bacon and Parmesan Omelet Pie, 42, **43**
Lemon Chess Pie with Cardamom, 200
Sweet Potato and Pecan Pie, **190,** 191
Pimento Cheese Biscuits, 28, **29**
Pineapple Upside-Down Cake, Fresh Fruit, 192
pineapple juice in Big Dipper Cocktail, **226,** 227
Pinto Bean Bowl with Fatback Corn Bread Crumble and Onion Jam, 124–125, **125**
piquillo peppers in Asparagus and Sweet Pepper Salad, 86
place, sense of, 100–101
Plum and Nectarine Yogurt Bowl with Wildflower Honey Granola, 47
pork. *See also* bacon; ham
Corn Bread and Pickle-Crusted Bone-In Spiral Cut Ham, 154, **155**
Country-Style Pork Spare Ribs, 133
potatoes. *See also* sweet potatoes
Mashed Potatoes and Turnips with Thyme Butter, **148,** 149
Onion Potatoes, 106

Shrimp Potato Salad, 130
Tangy Potato Salad, 94
Pound Cake, Goat Cheese, 184, **185**
Prime Rib Roast with Yorkshire Pudding, 156
provolone cheese in Collards and Italian Sausage Lasagna, 130, **131,** 132
Pumpkin Frosting, 178–179, **179**
Punch, Orange Cream, **210,** 211, **211**
Purple Hull Peas and Corn, 101

raspberries
Cantaloupe and Raspberries Milkshake, 208
Sweet Bread with Raspberries, 189
red onions
Chilled Cucumber Soup with Smoked Salmon, 74
Sardine and Cream Cheese Spread, 64, **65**
Shrimp Croquettes with Remoulade Coleslaw on a Bun, 137, **138,** 139
Strawberry, Romaine, and Red Onion Salad, 84, **85**
Tangy Potato Salad, 94
Watermelon Salad, 78
relish
Arugula and Egg Salad Tea Sandwiches, 169, **171**
Ham-Stuffed Eggs, 68
Shrimp Croquettes with Remoulade Coleslaw on a Bun, 137, **138,** 129
Shrimp Potato Salad, 136
Tangy Potato Salad, 94
ricotta cheese in Collards and Italian Sausage Lasagna, 130, **131,** 132
Ritz Crackers, Ham Terrine with, 62
Roast, Prime Rib, with Yorkshire Pudding, 156
Robinson, Addie, 166–167
Rolls, Buttermilk Yeast, 157
romaine lettuce
Caesar Salad with Arugula and Garlic Croutons, **82,** 83
Strawberry, Romaine, and Red Onion Salad, 84, **85**
rum
Banana and Chocolate Coffee Cake with Rum Glaze, 41
Peanut Rum and Coke, 224, **225**

Salads
Asparagus and Sweet Pepper Salad, 86
Beet, Apricot, and Goat Cheese Salad, **76,** 77
Caesar Salad with Arugula and Garlic Croutons, **82,** 83
Grape and Walnut Salad, 79
Iceberg Wedges with Cucumbers and Black Forest Ham, 80, **81**
Shrimp Potato Salad, 130
Strawberry, Romaine, and Red Onion Salad, 84, **85**
Watermelon Salad, 78
salami in Shrimp and Salami Egg Scramble, 33
salmon
Chilled Cucumber Soup with Smoked Salmon, 74
Pecan and Herb-Crusted Salmon, 135
sandwiches
Arugula and Egg Salad Tea Sandwiches, 169, **171**
Carolina Burger, 122–123, **123**
Cucumber and Jalapeño Tea Sandwiches, 168, **171**
Monte Cristo Sandwich, **36,** 37
Shrimp Croquettes with Remoulade Coleslaw on a Bun, 137, **138,** 139
Tomato and Shrimp Butter Tea Sandwiches, 170, **171**
Sardine and Cream Cheese Spread, 64, **65**
sausage
Collard and Italian Sausage Lasagna, 130, **131,** 132
Smothered Fried Chicken with Andouille Sausage, 116–117
Scones, Gorgonzola and Walnut, **172,** 173
seafood. *See also* salmon; shrimp
Caesar Salad with Arugula and Garlic Croutons, **82,** 83
Hot Crab Dip, 63
Sardine and Cream Cheese Spread, 64, **65**
sense of place, 100–101
shrimp
Grits Casserole with Shrimp Gravy, **30,** 31
Shrimp and Salami Egg Scramble, 33
Shrimp Croquettes with Remoulade Coleslaw on a Bun, 137, **138,** 139
Shrimp Potato Salad, 130
Tomato and Shrimp Butter Tea Sandwiches, 170, **171**
Smothered Fried Chicken with Andouille Sausage, 116–117
Snacks and Starters, 49–68
BLT Crackers, **60,** 61
Cheddar Cheese Relish, 58, **59**
Fresh Okra Fritters, **66,** 67
Fried Chicken Lollipops with Andalouse Sauce, 50, **51–53**
Ham-Stuffed Eggs, 68
Ham Terrine with Ritz Crackers, 62
Hot Crab Dip, 63
Sardine and Cream Cheese Spread, 64, **65**
Spiced Cocktail Peanuts, **56,** 57
Sweet Potato Corn Bread, 54

Soups
  Chilled Cucumber Soup with Smoked Salmon, 74
  Cream of Asparagus Soup with Mushroom Ragù, 70–71, **71**
  Cream of Turnip Soup with Crispy Greens, 75
sour cream
  Chilled Cucumber Soup with Smoked Salmon, 74
  Coconut Cake with Coconut Sour Cream Frosting, 177
  Grape and Walnut Salad, 79
  Tangy Potato Salad, 94
  Yellow Layer Cake with Pumpkin Frosting, 178–179, **179**
Southern Comfort in Big Dipper Cocktail, **226**, 227
Southern Foodways Alliance, 23
Southern New Year's Day meal, 152
Spiced Cocktail Peanuts, **56**, 57
Spinach, Parmesan, and Artichoke Gratin, **104**, 105
Stewed Corn, **92**, 93
strawberries
  Strawberry, Romaine, and Red Onion Salad, 84, **85**
  Strawberry Biscuit Cake, **182**, 183
String Beans with Fresh Herbs, 102, **103**
sunflower seeds in Plum and Nectarine Yogurt Bowl with Wildflower Honey Granola, 47
Sweet Bread with Raspberries, 189
Sweet Neecy Cake Mix Company, 23, 238
sweet potatoes
  Grated Sweet Potato Pancakes, 38, **39**
  Sweet Potato and Apple Bake, 107
  Sweet Potato and Pecan Pie, **190**, 191
  Sweet Potato Corn Bread, 54
  Sweet Potato Custard Ice Cream, 204, **205**
  Sweet Potato Hot Cross Buns, 147
Sweet Tea & Cornbread, 23, 238, 240
Swiss Chard and Chickpea Bread and Butter Pudding, 153
Swiss cheese in Monte Cristo Sandwich, **36**, 37

table setting, 158–159, **159**
Talley, André Leon, 93
Tangy Potato Salad, 94
tea parties, 166–167
thrift shopping, 55
timeline, 22–23
tomatoes. *See also* grape tomatoes; green tomatoes
  BLT Crackers, **60**, 61
  Eggplant and Tomato Casserole, 126
  Fried Green Tomato Parmesan, 121
  Tomato and Shrimp Butter Tea Sandwiches, 170, **171**
Tonya's Café, 23, 240
Tonya's Cookies, 12, 23, 240
Tonya's Pecan Crisp Cookies, 23
triple sec in Chapel Hill Cocktail, **228**, 229
Turkey, Fried, with Giblet Gravy, Mortadella Corn Bread Dressing, and Cranberry Compote, **160**, 161–163, **164**, **165**
turnips
  Cream of Turnip Soup with Crispy Greens, 75
  Mashed Potatoes and Turnips with Thyme Butter, **148**, 149

Umstead Park, 44

Vegetable Sides, 87–108
  Apple Coleslaw, **98**, 99
  Braised Collard Greens, 90, **91**
  Brûléed Corn Pudding, 108
  Country-Fried Cabbage, 95
  Macaroni and Cheese, 96, **97**
  Onion Potatoes, 106
  Purple Hull Peas and Corn, 101
  Spinach, Parmesan, and Artichoke Gratin, **104**, 105
  Stewed Corn, **92**, 93
  String Beans with Fresh Herbs, 102, **103**
  Sweet Potato and Apple Bake, 107
  Tangy Potato Salad, 94

walnuts
  Fried Walnuts, 144, **145**
  Gorgonzola and Walnut Scones, **172**, 173
  Grape and Walnut Salad, 79
  Plum and Nectarine Yogurt Bowl with Wildflower Honey Granola, 47
Watermelon Salad, 78
Williams, Albert (cousin of Spring), 22, 218
Williams, Larry (cousin of Spring), 229
Willing Workers, 220

Yellow Layer Cake with Pumpkin Frosting, 178–179, **179**
yogurt in Plum and Nectarine Yogurt Bowl with Wildflower Honey Granola, 47
Yorkshire Pudding, 156

Zucchini and Tomato Frittata, 34